The Impact of Technology

on

Behavior & Happiness

W0010876

Palmer

FIRST EDITION

Cover design by *Fantasyart*

United States of America Copyright registration 1-2169432921

Simendinger, Theodore John. Author.

The Impact of Technology on Behavior & Happiness/Theodore John Simendinger as "Ocean Palmer." 1st edition.

ISBN: 978-0-9765485-7-7

10 9 8 7 6 5 4 3 2 1

AIRPLANE READER PUBLISHING COMPANY

Denver, Colorado USA

ISBN Registration:

978-0-9765485-7-7 (print)

978-0-9765485-8-5 (eBook)

978-0-9765485-9-3 (others)

ELECTRONIC LICENSE NOTES

Dedication

To absent friends Jason Balatico, Ford Kanehira, Ronald Kawamae, Melvin Lee, Peter Mark, John Sakamoto, and Ronald Kataoka.

And to everyone who chooses to be positive in the lives of others.

Table of Contents

Meet the Author

Creator of 16 books and motion picture screenplays, Ocean Palmer is the *nom de plume* for multiple award-winning author and behaviorist Ted Simendinger.

An inspiring communicator of timely and relevant behavioral-based research, the Ocean Palmer brand deftly mixes modern ingredients. A life skills specialist, Ocean teaches head management, people development, and business problem solving. He uses simple explanations, heartfelt coaching, and heavy doses of inspiration to teach and entertain his audiences.

A professional humorist, Ocean is a popular media guest and one of the USA's top teaching experts on the subject of Worry. His popular book *Managing the Worry Circle (How to Improve Your Life by Worrying Less)* led to appearances on every major American television network and radio programs broadcast on thousands of stations around the world.

Long a supporter of higher education and inspired by alarming campus behavioral trends, Ocean researched and wrote *The Impact of Technology on Behavior & Happiness* to explain the seductive lure of digital addiction, why heads are increasingly crowded, and why patience and attention spans are shortening. He also uses in-depth research findings to explain the pluses and minuses of social media, along with an inside look at technology's product and marketing plans to continue modifying human behaviors.

More importantly, in addition to explaining what's going on and why, Ocean shares instantly usable tips so readers can create immediate, positive behavioral change.

Born in Philadelphia, Ocean Palmer grew up in Severna Park, Maryland. He attended college in northeast Florida and graduated from Jacksonville University as a business major with a triple minor in psychology, economics, and marketing. A brief stint as a newspaperman was followed by a distinguished 20-year career with Xerox Corporation. He left on the Millennium to follow his passion for helping people with crowded heads better manage their cranial air space.

His progressive research on the changing dynamics of human behavior has enabled Ocean to teach and lecture in more than 40 countries on six continents. *The Impact,* his fourth life skills book, follows in his life skills tradition of straight-talk explanation and enhanced self-awareness.

Ocean enjoys fishing, reading, golf, baseball, and walking his dogs. None requires a computer or phone but each provides private "think time," a block of which he incorporates into every day.

The author is always happy to hear from book clubs and readers, so if something in *The Impact* inspires a comment, feel free to visit his website at www.OceanPalmer.com and drop him a note. He promises to respond.

Foreword

I began studying the subject of worry more than three decades ago and interviewed over 4,000 people worldwide about what they worried about and why. Many of the key takeaways from that work are included in the "What to Do Today" section of this book.

As you dive in, be patient digesting the back-story. The framing of the economic and technological baselines that paved the highway for today's radically changed behaviors comprises the first third of *The Impact* ("Where We Were"), and methodically lays out the springboard from which we accelerate.

My research across the spectrum of other behavioral impact factors that expand the breadth and depth of *The Impact* dates back to late 1999. Shared below is the chilling story that sparked this important work.

Honolulu, Hawaii

November 2, 1999

It was 8:30 in the morning when I opened my ocean-view hotel room door at Oahu's Hilton Hawaiian Village to head down and catch a cab for a nine o'clock meeting on Bishop Street. The hotel phone rang. I paused in the doorway, debating whether or not to re-enter and answer. I had a half-hour, more than enough time for a three-mile cab ride, so I pivoted back inside and picked up the telephone.

That two-minute conversation, initiated by a co-worker I barely knew, changed my life forever.

"I'm so glad I got you," she said. "We have to cancel our meeting."

"How come?"

"We had a bit of a tragedy this morning. Have you seen the news?"

"No." I rarely watch TV and never in the morning so I asked what happened.

"One of the technicians shot seven others at a team meeting. He's still on the loose. A SWAT team is here and they want us to disperse in case he's headed this way (the main Xerox office)."

The shootings had occurred just 30 minutes earlier, at 8 a.m., in a parts warehouse where Xerox repairmen met each morning before fanning throughout the paved veins of Oahu to repair the copy machines that had broken down the day before.

The nondescript two-story building where the shootings took place was on the east side on Nimitz Highway, the main drag between the Honolulu Airport and Waikiki. Virtually every tourist visiting Honolulu has driven past.

Stunned, I pulled the phone away from my left ear and studied it before responding. I had no idea what to say, so we agreed to exchange voice mails later in the day and figure out what to do. In the meantime, I was told to stay away.

Where I ended up dispersing was a side street of antique shops on the fringe of Waikiki, about 600 yards from where the gunman would later be apprehended. I mindlessly window-shopped, staring at everything but seeing only my reflection. I bought nothing except a badly burnt cup of coffee that tasted like diesel sipped from a styrofoam cup. I struggled to reconcile the abrupt savagery of this hideous human tragedy.

As the story unfolded, details made it worse. A 15-year employee, the shooter feared his recent job performance would be a topic of morning discussion with his peers, a worry compounded by the impending release of an entire new line of electronically enhanced products he doubted he could learn. Machines to that point were electromechanical and subject to frequent breakdowns. New production devices would rely much more on complicated electronic circuitry, which would improve reliability but demand a steep technical learning curve. Technological design advancements caused the change, which was celebrated by salespeople but worrisome to repairmen.

At the time, the shooter was a member of what Xerox called a "self-managed work group." Each team faced a pooled collection of service calls that was left to them to divide. If everyone pulled his or her weight—the theoretical concept design—the work was completed with everyone contributing equally. If customers were satisfied, and the work was evenly divided and cost-contained, the team was successful.

But if someone did not perform what was perceived as his or her fair share, he or she faced a worse punishment than getting hollered at by a boss. No one wanted to face a room of critical, disapproving teammates.

In the days that followed the shootings I heard different versions of the gunman's situation. One was that he was underperforming and feared for his job. Another was that he wasn't slacking and was, in the words of HR, simply a "troubled employee."

Opinions are not facts and the company line was designed, drawn, and communicated to protect the privacy of the principals involved.

Two days after the carnage I heard firsthand from the wife of one of the victims that her husband had voiced a fearful concern over breakfast coffee that the shooter was going to snap and do something drastic. One hour later her husband was proved correct, sprawled dead on the office floor in a seeping pool of blood.

All seven victims were men who worked on the largest machines Xerox made, the big, fast, world-class production devices. While a salesman might spend a month or six or twelve getting a customer to buy, the technician had to ensure the machine's reliability. Sales saw a customer a few times, got the order, scooped up a commission check, and moved on to cut another deal. The repairman, based on one call per-week, which was common at the time, would see the client 250 times over the product's useful life.

Because the big machines generated the greatest amount of revenue and profit, they were the most important products Xerox sold, which made the technicians' work vitally important. The service organization was the backbone of Xerox Hawaii.

For a fellow like me—a 20-year sales executive—the thought that a co-worker in such a team-centric corporate culture could systematically eradicate the lives of seven men he had worked with for 15 years was unfathomable. Every reason I considered seemed to bounce off logic like a raindrop on a waxed automobile. None sunk in.

Xerox had about 150 employees across all islands, mostly on Oahu. The gunman wiped out five percent in a matter of minutes. Five died in a conference room, the other two in front of their PCs in an adjoining office area. The gunman chose not to shoot another sitting nearby. His twentieth and final shot missed an eighth potential victim, who raced to escape down a stairwell.

After the shootings, the gunman calmly walked out to his green service van, drove out the back lot, and waved to the parking lot attendant as he pulled onto Nimitz Highway and disappeared into rush hour traffic.

Within minutes the story was all over the news and blanketed the island. At 3 o'clock, tipped off by a woman jogger who had heard an all-points radio bulletin, the police found the shooter sitting in his van in a quiet, peaceful park. They took him into custody without resistance.

Within 24 hours a team of company human resources professionals had flown over, set up trust funds, insurance plans, college funds—everything they could think of to remove potential downstream financial stress from the lives of stricken survivors.

Money for these families would not be a problem. Nor would it provide solace.

The following morning, two days after the shootings, three senior Xerox executives flew over from the mainland. The new CEO, brought in from the outside a couple years before, knew little of the Xerox corporate culture and proved it. He began his address to the assembled Oahu employees by talking about how Xerox "didn't have a policy" for such a tragedy and that he had been busy helping create one, the specifics of which he couldn't get into. Later in his speech, which ended in less than 15 minutes, he stumbled through the names of the seven victims, mispronouncing several.

I stood along the back wall and closed my eyes when the CEO fumbled the men's names. Every mistake was a needle in the eye of decency to the 100-plus people sitting before him in folding chairs, grief-stricken friends and associates who had invested their careers alongside these innocent, hardworking victims.

Not only did this outsider not understand the company's culture, he also did not understand island culture. Love and kindness for family, friends, and acquaintances are the soul of Hawaii.

When it was the turn of the local general manager to speak, the words would not come out. I had never, and still have never, felt so sorry for someone so good, a man who tried so hard to make things better for all people under his watch. This fellow, a young and talented man, had dealt a couple years prior with having his chest cracked open after suffering a premature heart attack. His leadership focus was on the community, his passion to make the islands better for all. And now this.

Here we were, two days removed, and here he stood—knowing that one of his people committed the most heinous crime in the history of the Hawaiian statehood—trying but unable to complete a full sentence in a halting, broken, trembling voice.

An island reverend, a bear of a man, followed. He brought measured calm to the audience by speaking in a slow, deep, and kindly reassuring voice about living lives of righteous decency. He said lives are houses built on sand or stone, delivering his message in a manner that seemed all too familiar with bereavement.

In outstretched hands he held a vine, a special vine that only grows in a special rocky cliff on one side of the island. It was a healing vine with beautiful flowers of orchid-like beauty. This special vine, he said, makes its home, and thrives, in a foundation of stone.

After the ceremony, grief counselors were available for anyone seeking support. I went on a customer call instead. The call ended up as you might expect, empty and unfulfilling, since I did not care and did not want to be there. One of the people with me had a lot of money and an award trip waiting if we got the order. Money and trips were nowhere on the radar of my heart or soul. Seven men had died—seven husbands, fathers, and sons stolen—all because they went to work on time, just like they were supposed to.

The gunman, on the surface, had a profile that the news media speculated offered clues he might snap. He was 40, lived at home under the subservient thumb of his father and older brother, and had no wife or children. He had been on the high school shooting team and owned 17 guns.

There is virtually nowhere to hunt in Hawaii, save for turkeys on one of the islands, and his permit request for an 18th gun had been denied several years prior after a hot-tempered altercation in a customer's office, after which he damaged an elevator that cost his father $1,500 in reparations.

When word of the shootings reached the gunman's father, the father's comment was that his son had caused him to lose face and that he wished his son had one bullet remaining so he could finish the job (by killing himself).

It did not seem to be a household of love that spat this angry man from society into a jail cell, and his innocent-by-reason-of-insanity plea was rejected. He was found guilty of murder and sentenced to life imprisonment without parole.

Aside from shooting his guns at the range, the gunman's hobbies included raising koi (tropical carp), making and refinishing furniture, and fixing cars, all of which involved silent or inanimate objects. Nothing he did involved supportive human interactions.

His job, frustrating by its very nature, was to fix broken things in environments where impatient customers often depended upon the machine to finish their work and earn their livelihood. I was told that he believed people sabotaged his machines by breaking them on purpose, going so far as to hide on occasion to watch and see. No one was found to be doing so.

Eventually, it seems, life's pressures became too much. No man can live without friends, or love and respect, and his life seemed absent of all. The internalized frustrations of a quiet, defeated 40-year-old man grew in pressure until finally exploding like the volcano on the nearby Big Island, lava flowing from the fingertips of a warm-barreled 9-millimeter.

After my customer meeting that morning after the CEO's bungled speech, I returned to my hotel and changed clothes, then went for a long run in the rain on what was an unusually dark and nasty day in paradise.

I wanted to run until my legs were too heavy to run any farther. Running gave me time to think about many things as I watched surfers by the jetty and continued past the Waikiki Yacht Club harbor where, like everywhere, flags flew at half-mast.

I ran through a park, past the fishing boats and Ala Moana, and almost as far as the building on Nimitz, which in a matter of minutes on a dreary Tuesday morning changed from an anonymous warehouse to the furnace of Hell.

I purposefully turned around before reaching the building, believing it served no ghoulish purpose to be counted among the curious. As I looped back, directly into the rainy headwind, I was transfixed by the majesty of Diamondhead standing so high and mighty in the distance. I swore I could see my seven fallen co-workers standing at the peak, side-by-side with their right arms raised high and waving, as if to let us know they were okay, that they were closer to the Lord and would find new lives as vines in the rock until it was time for their families to join them in the bosom of heaven.

May God continue to touch the heart, and kiss the soul, of all those scarred by this blood-spilled river of sorrow.

I am one of those forever changed by the irreversible anger of a broken man. I quit my job three weeks later, trading a safe future retirement for far more important work inspired by this awful tragedy. My charter in life is to help people stay balanced and happy.

All companies are good at some things but lousy at others and Xerox was no exception. My long history of senior-level interactions with leaders of famous brands from coast to coast seemed to underscore that making better people—resilient, self-motivated, and happy people—was an all too common shortcoming.

This, I believed, was fixable. I knew I could help others from reaching such hopeless depths of despair by helping them understand the interlocking relationships of cause and effect, emotion and worry management, and generating confidence from behavioral awareness.

This book builds upon the international acceptance of my work in the field of worry by incorporating the effects of two additional things, the emotional and financial impact of the recession, plus the increasing permeation of technology, which is rapidly and radically changing behaviors around the globe for better and worse.

Technological inventions and advancements march to market relentlessly, in many cases faster than people can comfortably keep up. There are a lot of crowded heads out there, and too many frustrated people.

Far more important than summarizing facts, this book shares *solutions*. Readers will learn what is going on behaviorally and why, and how to regain control of their personal air space to make better, more confident behavioral choices.

When we understand why we do what we do, and feel the way we do, and possess the necessary emotional tools to change behaviors when we know deep down we should, we are better equipped to find and maintain a life of positive, even-keeled contentment. These are life skills, and life skills come in handy regardless what new gadgets, apps, and digital enticements enter our lives.

Trust what you learn and share those insights with others. May you, and they, forever live in a safe and happy house of stone.

Introduction

On September 15, 2008, United States financial services titan Lehman Brothers filed for Chapter 11 bankruptcy protection. The collapse remains, by far, the largest implosion in U. S. economic history. Lehman's cooked books torched investors to the tune of an estimated $640 billion in assets.

To put this seismic shock in perspective, seven years prior, Enron—a Houston-based energy company— became a household dirty word when auditors discovered accounting fraud tied to $66 billion. Enron was chump change compared to Lehman Brothers. Lehman's shenanigans were ten times worse.

Seven weeks after Lehman collapsed, Barack Obama was elected the 44th president of the United States. This was a historic for a couple reasons, one being his ethnicity. The other was Obama's smart, strategic use of emerging technology to expand his voter base and raise money.

Obama was the first presidential candidate to parlay the effective use of the Internet to inform and persuade voters. His opponent, John McCain, eschewed the tool and relied on traditional campaign practices.

Obama's different approach to influencing electorate behavior was lauded by sales industry professionals. In October, just weeks prior to his election, Obama was voted *Advertising Age* magazine's "Marketer of the Year." Among those Obama trumped for the honor were Apple and Zappos.com, a pair of indisputable marketing powerhouses.

Soon after the election, *Advertising Age* ran an analysis of the Obama advertising and outreach campaign. The magazine lauded the president's team for their "understanding of ground-level marketing strategies and tactics, everything from audience segmentation and database management to the creation and maintenance of online communities."

When Obama took office in January, two things were apparent: The world was in a financial mess, and technology's role in shaping opinion and behaviors was indisputable. In many regards, the Obama campaign dawned of a new era.

The Impact of Technology on Behaviors & Happiness is segmented into four sections:

1. *Where We Were*, which frames recession and technology's impact on behavior and life since 2008.

2. *Where We Are*. As the slow economic recovery continues, and technology expands throughout our daily lives, we examine specific behaviors that have

decreased and increased in frequency, and analyze what these changes mean to self-image, self-esteem, happiness, and contentment. We also discuss technology's role in 2016 politics, which I call "The Summer of Discontent."

3. *Where We Are Headed* looks forward at future trends and their impact on interactive communities of tomorrow.

4. *What to Do Today.* This section shares a comprehensive life skills coaching guide for those struggling with happiness, frustration, or the pursuit of contentment in an increasingly digital world.

The book links the explosion of technology since Barack Obama's first presidential election to how and why technology has so radically changed behavior, and will continue to exert its muscles for more change for better and worse.

For those feeling squeezed by technology's ever-lengthening tentacles, also included are tips for easily "doable" techniques to help manage these changing behaviors and increase happiness.

I often say that the more gadgets we invent to simplify our lives, the more complicated it seems to become. Life need not be that way. If you feel sometimes that your tools are managing you, instead of you managing them, there are specific behavioral reasons you feel that way.

The book shares solutions, so embrace and share what you learn. Fix or change what's required and pay it forward by coaching those you care about.

Too many crowded heads perch upon the shoulders of unhappy and discontent people walking among us. Their numbers are increasing, as is digital addiction.

When we understand the impact of technology on behavior and happiness, we are better prepared to protect ourselves and remain in a happier, more positive place. Insight and understanding also deliver a bonus: We become far better coaches when assisting those in need.

Navigating life is a personal pursuit that, at times, is very much a team sport. Take care of yourself, and help others along the way.

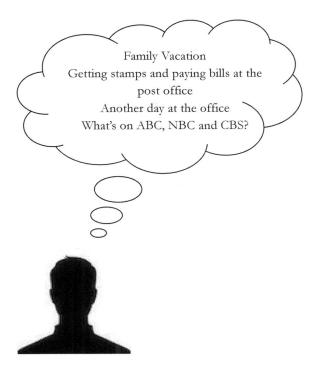

The Old Days

In the old days, back before technology took over, life was simpler to navigate because heads were uncluttered.

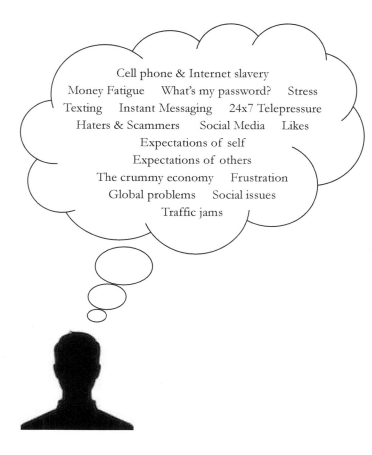

Modern Days

Nowadays, things seem far more complicated.

But why?

Perhaps it's best to start when the economy collapsed in 2008.

Chapter 1

Where We Were

The Economy

Prior to the economic collapse of 2008, life was pretty good. People were working, money was flowing, and phantom equity in home ownership kept rising. People were dining out, buying cars, shopping, and traveling. Our thoughts focused more on wealth accumulation than job security. We had jobs; we wanted more money.

Few knew that we were standing at cliff's edge of the longest economic run-up in American history. Most of us took the economy for granted, assuming that because cash came easily it always would. We wanted more toys. After all, we are Americans and Americans like new and shiny things.

But things changed seemingly overnight. A disastrous recession spread like windswept fire through a tinder-dry, deadwood forest. Powerhouse companies toppled like dominoes. Starbucks shuttered 600 locations in America and 60 more in Australia. Bennigans went under. Fast casual restaurants lost their sit-down-and-tip clientele to cheaper fast food drive-thru chains.

The Big Six car manufacturers were slammed by a trifecta of badness: high gas prices, shrinking home equity, and nervous consumers. The auto industry had its worst results in 16 years. Year-over-year unit sales for Ford, GM, and Chrysler were all down, dropping between 20-and-30 percent. Japanese manufacturers Toyota, Honda, and Nissan were also off but only half as much as their American competitors.

The retail sector got punched even harder. The *New York Times* reported retail sales plummeted to its lowest level in 35 years. Retailer reactions were all over the board, making this an especially interesting sector for economists to watch.

Department store revenues dropped 13.3 percent, with specialty apparel dropping 10.4 percent. Merchants took various approaches to deal with recessional reality. If a company discounted heavily, it could move merchandise. If it did not, their inventory collected dust. During Christmas season high-end apparel was discounted 70 percent—heretofore an unheard of pricing strategy.

Retailers who moved product at whatever price necessary at least generated cash and cleaned out inventory. Those who didn't got crushed. Unless you were Walmart, which was perfectly positioned, this was a brutal time for retailing.

Walmart had expanded offerings and aggressively priced brand-name merchandise from names like Sony and Samsung, a strategy move that paid off beautifully. Customers who had never stepped inside a Walmart suddenly showed up to spend and save big.

Walmart sold a tremendous volume of product, feeding a demand so strong one of their workers in New York was trampled to death in a customer stampede when the doors flung open on Black Friday.

Although shopping patterns shifted and consumers saved money by cutting corners, most opted not to go on their normal vacations. More than half of families (57 percent) cancelled or cut back on travel expenditures and opted to stay home. More than half the nation found itself with extra hours to watch TV and surf the Internet.

While America's economy was getting pummeled from pillar to post, we were not alone. Many countries around the world saw their economies crumble and millions upon millions of good, hardworking people were thrown out of work. Only a few developed nations (such as Poland and Slovakia) were spared. South Korea and Australia wobbled slightly. China and India escaped the worst of it too, as their conservative economies were also more cash-based than fueled by leveraged mortgages and borrowed money. Africa was unaffected since its natural resources were going to China and its nations were not fully integrated in the world market.

America was different. We were leveraged to the eyeballs, poster children for borrowed debt, with embarrassingly poor financial governance controls.

As a result, American household debt was way too high. Measured as a percentage of annual disposable personal income, family debt loads in December 2007 were 127 percent. In other words, for every four available dollars we had in hand to spend, we spent five.

This risky debt level was a full 50 percent higher than 1990, when financial lending regulations were tighter and borrowed money was harder to get. Since America is a consumer-driven society, when we had access to money we took it. And when we took it, we spent it.

Other countries did too. According to the International Monetary Fund (IMF) in April 2012, "Household debt soared in the years leading up to the downturn. In advanced economies, during the five years preceding 2007, the ratio of household debt to income rose by an average of 39 percentage points, to 138 percent."

Some countries found themselves even worse off. Denmark, Iceland, Ireland, the Netherlands, and Norway saw debt soar to more than 200 percent of household income. Historic highs in household debt also occurred in emerging economies such as Estonia, Hungary, Latvia, and Lithuania.

The IMF drew European parallels to America.

"The concurrent boom in both house prices and the stock market meant that household debt relative to assets held broadly stable," they wrote, "which masked households' growing exposure to a sharp fall in asset prices.

"When house prices declined, ushering in the global financial crisis, many households saw their wealth shrink relative to their debt, and, with less income and more unemployment, found it harder to meet mortgage payments.

"By the end of 2011, real house prices had fallen from their peak by about 41 percent in Ireland, 29 percent in Iceland, 23 percent in Spain (same as the United States), and 21 percent in Denmark."

Household defaults, underwater mortgages (where the loan balance exceeded the house value), foreclosures, and fire sales were widespread. Millions of stressed out, desperate people and households were forced to deleverage by paying off debts or defaulting on obligations and home ownership.

This was most pronounced in the United States, where defaults became the primary means of debt reduction. Giving up constituted two-thirds of American debt solutions.

The Emotional Problems of Mass Uncertainty

Without predictability, or some sort of realistic floor about how bad *bad* was going to be, millions of scared workers—plus the worried unemployed—hunkered down. Because bills stood so tall for so many, stress jitters caused millions to pay down debt rather than spend. Paying down debt is not as much fun as accumulating new toys, but forced austerity called for less glamorous choices and the frugal majority minimized risk and cut back on non-essential consumption.

Cognitively they changed and behaviorally they changed, trading their previous "I want it" attitude for "I don't need it" fiscal conservatism. According to Pew Research, 71 percent of families bought less expensive brands, 62 percent cut back on household spending, and 30 percent cut back on personal vices like booze and cigarettes.

Uncertainty also influenced job market behaviors. Unhappy people stayed in a job because at least they had a bad one to go to. Everyone had friends and colleagues who had lost their jobs, and few were willing to risk a known paycheck when no one seemed to be hiring.

Second, new jobs were slow to be created because people were paying down or walking away from debt rather than consuming. Since additional workers are needed only when goods and services are in demand, rather than chase top-line revenue growth, most employers cut below-the-line expenses. Instead of hiring staff and adding to overhead and headcount, employers dumped more work on existing staff. Worker stress levels skyrocketed.

Employers held the hammer. They could cut salaries, modify pension plans, increase pressure and workloads, and reduce benefits. Workers were relatively powerless. The worker had one option: leave. But in a dead job market with millions looking for work, few were willing to jump.

From a work force composition standpoint, America's plurality of workers was comprised of Baby Boomers, 60 million of them closing in on their hoped-for retirement. Fifty-five million Gen Xers patiently (and impatiently) waited for those positions. Fledgling

Millennials were in no hurry to leave college and search haystacks for job needles.

The recession squashed promotion hopes. Retirement stock and investment funds were crushed, so millions of Boomers found themselves economic hostages, unexpectedly forced to keep working in order to rebuild adequate retirement wealth.

With Boomers bottlenecking the top of the traditional corporate career escalator, talented Gen Xers found their careers stuck in neutral. Too many Boomers stayed on the job for too many extra years, which froze career escalations.

The Behavioral Impact

Forced austerity torpedoed the American psyche and sank it to a darkly negative place, so the national mood was predictably glum.

Prior to the recession, the number one worry of consumer-driven Americans was wealth accumulation. The crash changed that biggest worry almost overnight to having, holding onto, or finding a job. Endless layoff-related news reports permeated the airwaves and work-related stress mushroomed toward an all-consuming 24/7 obsession.

Too many could not cope with the darkness. Multiple major news outlets on both sides of the Atlantic, among them National Public Radio and CBS, reported than an additional 10,000 people more than normal-many of them middle-aged-committed suicide. While this is a comparative trend statistic of fact, it is also impossible to truly understand the precise reason or reasons anyone chooses to take his or her life.

Technology

Thanks to LCD screens and flat-screens, televisions were still the digital gorilla of recreational choice. But when the recession hit, TV sales slowed. With discretionary spending limited due to a frugal conscience born of tight money, large screen purchases (40+ inches) grew just three percent. Shipments of all LCD televisions dropped to less than half of what they were during the previous six quarters. Big box stores couldn't move inventory and off-brand manufacturers went out of business. Except for the affluent, television purchases were made with tight money based on need-not want.

Computers

As technology continued to evolve and grab increasingly greater amounts of consumer attention, the other stationary targets besides televisions where customers voted with their wallets were desktop computers.

In mature markets like North America and Europe, who were far advanced with familiarity and saturation as opposed to emerging markets such as China or Africa, computer purchases were generally replacement upgrades. In emerging markets purchases were net additions to the population.

Tablets were relatively new on the scene but soon became, by far, the fastest growing segment. Despite launching into the force of the recession, unit totals doubled in five years. Between the recession's onset in 2008 and 2016, sales trebled, with the most dramatic growth coming from portable devices customized for personal utility.

Back when the recession struck, desktop computers and notebooks split 90 percent of the market. Today desktops hold a mere 18 percent of the market, while tablets, which did not arrive until 2010, hold a 23 percent share-a huge move underscoring the consumer preference for portability, convenience, personalization, and ease of use.

Despite the precipitous decline in desktop PC sales since 2008, notebook sales remain constant, as do mini PCs. Tablets-which were way more affordable than desktops-enabled customers the chance to add their flexibility and capability plus new, personally relevant technology such as a smartphone, accessories, and peripherals without increasing overall spend. Unit ownership mushroomed.

Email

Direct email messaging was invented in 1971 by 30-year-old computer programmer Ray Tomlinson, a New Yorker who figured out how to send computer-to-computer messages over DARPANET, the precursor to the Internet.

At the time, computers were rare and quite expensive. It would take two decades plus the development of the personal computer and pioneer online services such as America Online (AOL), Prodigy, and CompuServe to enable one of today's most popular communication techniques to gain traction.

Tomlinson was a problem solver, and the problem he wanted to sort out how was how to communicate with someone without the need for him or her to be attending their telephone.

"The telephone was fine," he said, "but someone had to be there to receive the call."

Back then answering machines were rare, so companies and people of means hired answering services to keep track of their calls. Email was destined to change all that way beyond what Tomlinson expected.

"I see email being used, by and large, exactly the way I envisioned," he said. "In particular, it's not strictly a work tool or strictly a personal thing. Everybody uses it in different ways, but they use it in a way they find works for them."

Email in 2008 versus today

When the recession hit in 2008, there were 1.3 billion email keybeaters worldwide, which represented nearly two-thirds of all Internet users.

By 2015 emailers had doubled and users will continue to grow as the world outside America and Europe continues to show relentless online gains.

Despite alternative digital communications channels that move billions of additional messages via alternative means, email remains the primary communication channel of global business but a ceilinged one among individual users.

Today three-fourths of the world's 4.6 billion email accounts are consumer accounts. Personal email send-

and-receives are trending down three percent per year, due largely to social networking sites, text messaging, mobile instant messaging, and other technology-based alternatives that provide personal touch immediacy.

To use social networking sites a user must have an email account, so these will rise although message traffic often routes through alternative channels.

Business email is increasing

While personal email use has crested and is tapering down slightly, business email continues its dramatic and ominous rise. Business email quantities grow approximately seven percent each year. With one billion business email boxes feeding the frenzy and cloud accessibility keeping everyone within reach and on call, business use will continue to fuel mailbox growth and email utilization. Traffic numbers are staggering:

- Over 100 billion business related emails are sent and received daily.

- By the end of 2017, this number is expected to rise to 137 billion.

- The digital blizzard means that the average worker-who currently sends and receives 121 emails per day-will be wrestling with 140 per day within the next two years.

Industry research consultants The Ranicati Group point out that even though spam blockers are far more sophisticated now than back in 2008-when 70 percent of emails were spam-business emails steadily climb.

Websites, Spam & Viruses

Websites are usually designed to generate interest, action, and interaction. From 2008-2014 they skyrocketed from 188 million to over *one billion,* a number that seems unfathomable since the average online user visits just 96 separate domains per month.

A common function of many sites is to collect user traffic data using far more sophisticated methods than those available during the recession. Advertising and emails, often unsolicited, track and follow site-jumping visitors.

Spam went from an angry but rare annoyance back in 2001-when a mere eight percent of email was identified that way-to a colossal pain in the butt in 2006-2007. Botnets turned inboxes into outhouses, as spam rates soared above 80 percent before peaking at 89.1 percent in 2010. When three of the kingpin botnets-Rustock, Lethic, and Xarvester-were halted, and the gangs responsible for pharmaceutical spam blizzards fractured, spam rates finally subsided. The biggest spammers pushed sex and dating, pills, jewelry, and weight loss.

Buried inside the sales messages were malware and phishing threats, which angered computer users even further. The recession year of 2008 saw roughly one million viruses. Six years later Money.com estimated that 2014's total was 317 million, roughly 800,000 per day.

The bigger the web and its global user group mushroomed, the more lucrative the rewards grew for increasing numbers of well organized cyber criminals. Viruses, financial scams, and other threats to privacy and security contributed to end user worry and frustration. But with email use becoming a normal part of daily life for billions, bad guys could move cyber pawns into place easier than ever. The tool shifted from naïve innocence to skeptical mistrust.

Contrasting the emotional experience of email: then vs. now

In its infancy, email was fun. Getting a few at work was a nice surprise, and responses typically invested time in thoughtful message crafting and careful review.

Today things are different. Response times vary by age demographic but gone are the days of instant reply.

Messages are getting shorter-statistically so by demographic-with brevity and emoticons replacing reflective composition. Most people are not gifted writers and lack command of the language, which technology is also statistically proving. What we lack in quality we make up for in quantity.

So while business increasingly relies on more emailed written words, it leans on areas beyond most employees' effective mastery. Replies are brief, at times cryptic, and often misinterpreted, misunderstood, or mistake-laden.

The chore of dealing with a cluttered inbox presents both a logistical and emotional burden. Few people leap out of bed and whistle their way to work to process and write 121 emails-today's daily average. Fewer still find inspiration, exhilaration, and personal fulfillment from staring at a screen for eight, nine, or ten exhausting hours. For those who get 200 or 300 a day, dealing with that many day after day can, in the words of my friend Steve Moore, "Suck the life right out of you."

As bad as this is, it shall worsen. Industry analysts project the weight of the email workload will grow seven percent heavier next year, an additional seven percent the year after, plus seven percent more the year after that.

Email used to be a supplemental means of communication but today is the primary communication tool of business, one that continues to detach millions from direct social interactions. Even if a worker replies to only half of what comes in, he or she still faces the relentless need to process something every ten minutes-just to keep up, much less get ahead.

Worldwide Internet use continues to escalate

A growth chart that showed the extraordinary rise of global Internet usage would resemble a tall, steep staircase. In 1993 virtually no one was online. Today, less than 25 years later, more than 40 percent of the world's 7.3 billion population has Internet access.

Two decades of double-digit growth pushed the world's online community from zilch to one billion in 2005, which at the time represented 15.8 percent of the global population. By 2008, when the recession hit, 1.5+ billion were online. Tight money or not, usage kept climbing.

By 2010 the global total of online users soared past two billion. In 2015, and despite the maturation of the American and European marketplaces, the world's online community surpassed three billion.

The multiplicative effect of the Internet's zooming global popularity is especially impressive when compared to the world's population growth rate, which holds fairly steady at 1.2 percent per year.

Five industrialized nations-the United States, Japan, Germany, France, and the United Kingdom-have greater than 85 percent Internet user penetration. The world's two population giants, China and India, have 46 percent and 19 percent respectively, figures that will continue growing at rapid rates.

With all signs pointing toward more email, the task-oriented nature of weeding a perpetually overgrown inbox garden places increasing time pressures, and emotional burdens, on everyone forced to do so.

Ray Tomlinson, the visionary inventor who placed the @ symbol in email addresses because, he said, "It was the only preposition on the keyboard," died in March 2016. He was pushing 75, and still working a corporate job for Raytheon.

The man who invented a handy tool of convenience and practical utility never intended to obsolete the telephone, he simply wanted to create an alternative to sitting by one.

Today seven trillion emails per year zoom around cyberspace, senders and receivers straddling an @ symbol, teaming to connect a rapidly shrinking world.

Cell phones

Apple's original iPhone was launched in 2007 and was an instant hit. In a mere 74 days customers purchased a million of them, each tied to AT&T, which was the unit's sole service provider.

A year later, in 2008, Apple released the iPhone 3. Consumer reaction was even stronger. Apple sold a million the first weekend, a remarkable acceptance and growth trend that would continue with every subsequent release. In 2009-during the worst of the recession-the iPhone 3GS needed just three days to sell a million.

Even as other notable suppliers entered the space, Nokia and Samsung among them, Apple's iPhone juggernaut controlled market share and revenue. Competitors were forced to sell at cost simply to stay in the game.

Apple had no such problem. Their profit margins reached upward of 75 percent and sales skyrocketed every quarter until Q4 of 2011 when, in a down quarter, they still sold in excess of 17 million.

With demand suppressed in expectation of the iPhone 4's release, once the new model became available sales exploded again. The iPhone 4 netted 600,000 pre-orders plus 1.7 million more within three days of availability. The iPhone 4s then buried all previous records, racking up one million presales and four million more sold within three days of launch. Apple sold 72 million iPhone 4s in six months.

Cheap, portable, and versatile, the iPhone line sold more units in its first five years than Apple's popular Mac computer line did in three decades.

The message to the marketplace was clear: The future was in little screens for personal convenience, not big ones parked on TV stands or medium-sized ones sitting on desktops.

Texting

Texting was invented on December 3, 1992 by 22-year-old Englishman Neil Papworth, a test engineer and developer on a team under contract to Vodaphone to create a SMSC (Shared Message Service Center). Because phones back then could not type (nor send) Neil typed and sent a message reading "Merry Christmas" from his computer to an early version cell phone on the Vodaphone network held by Vodaphone director Richard Jarvis, who was attending the office Christmas party.

Cell phone technology was primitive back then. The Tegic system-predictive word interpretation-was introduced in 1995 but it wasn't until Nokia launched a phone in 1997 that a full QWERTY keyboard was designed into the unit. Keys had to be depressed, as touch technology had not yet been invented.

This, of course, changed in 2007 when Apple introduced the touch screen-and with it-the modern "smartphone." Impending global recession or not, the innovative technology meant the previously gimmicky, occasional SMS could now become a far more efficient means of true interactive communication.

By 2009 teenagers were sending an average of 50 texts per day. Usage steadily climbed. Today texts outnumber phone calls and average out to about 700 per person per month. Frequency has somewhat flattened out, as other means of instant messaging can now be done online.

As for the inventor whose Christmas good wishes made him a folk hero in digital communication and truly changed how the world communicates, Neil Papworth and his family live quietly in Montreal, where he works on 4G initiatives for Oracle.

Gaming

Gaming experts Ulf Hagen and Södertörns Högskola of Tallinn University wrote extensively about the evolution of digital gaming, which grew from a humble, rudimentary beginning into what is today a massive industry.

Pong, an electronic action game played on a console by competing players, was the forerunner. Wildly popular when launched in 1972, players competed against each other in electronic Ping-Pong.

Two types of games would soon emerge, action games (like Pong) and thinking games. Both would expand into multiple derivative genres such as:

- Shoot 'em up

- Platform (multi-level) games

- Racing

- Sports

- Strategy

- Fighting

- Simulation

- Adventure

- Role-playing

- Puzzles and board games

- Edutainment

Because smartphone gaming had yet to come on the scene, back in 2008 competition raged between the PlayStation 3 and the Xbox 360, both of which were home devices. Barbara Ortutay of the Associated Press wrote about the state of the industry in January 2009, pointing out that although the economy was worsening, video games were selling at record levels.

"Grand Theft Auto IV" was the kingpin, racking up a commanding 44 percent of all sales.

But with the rise in aggression-oriented games came a larger social problem: increased youth violence. As Laurence Kulhner and Cheryl K. Olson documented in their fascinating book, *Grand Theft Childhood: The Surprising Truth about Violent Video Games and What Parents Can Do,* all four key metric area tied to school behavior-plus all 12 subset measurement areas-showed gamers to have roughly twice the problems of non-gamers.

Boy gamers were statistically worse than their female counterparts, but girl gamers also had significantly greater issues than their non-gaming counterparts in key measurement areas of grades, truancy, teacher trouble, and suspensions.

Kulhner and Olson's fact-based analysis suggested that the recession and technology expansion was negatively affecting far more than just the psyche of parental work and money problems. Problems at school created even more stressful problems at home. These gaming-centric behavioral complications piled additional stress onto millions of already unhappy, frustrated parents.

Facebook

When the recession hit, Facebook had less than 100 million users. Two years later the social media giant had 500 million. By September 2012, they passed one billion. Next year Facebook's social media empire will oversee a population that exceeds 1.5 billion.

In the Beginning

Back in late 2007, still finding its way as a small, private group, Facebook made a shrewd decision to springboard its growth by forging engagements with 2,000+ colleges and 25,000+ high schools. The youthful social network also branched out to feature 100,000 business pages, which allowed companies to share information and attract potential customers. With international reach expanding quickly, in October 2008 Facebook announced the opening of a global headquarters in Dublin, Ireland.

Less than three years later, during the summer of 2011, Facebook was the world's largest online photo host, cited by Facebook application and online photo aggregator Pixable as having 100 billion member-submitted photographs.

Mix an exploding smartphone market, where each new model introduced ever-improving camera technology, with tech-savvy Millennials who loved the social media concept, and Facebook founder Mark Zuckerberg had exactly what he wanted: a perfect fit with habitually engaged and action-oriented target customers.

Zuckerberg knew his audience and kept feeding them more of what they wanted. By October 2011, over 350 million users-nearly half of Facebook's 800 million total-accessed Facebook through their mobile phones. Smartphones let everyone stay in touch wherever they were and quickly accounted for one-third of all Facebook traffic.

Converting free to money

Having hired Sheryl Sandberg as Chief Operating Officer in March 2008, Zuckerberg let Sandberg recommend the company's best long term monetization strategy. After a series of meetings with employees, she concluded that advertising was the way to go. Ad-free during its building years but now with enormous critical mass and data-mining heft, Facebook changed its advertising model. The goal was simple: make money. Big money. The bigger, the better. Eighteen months after taking over as COO, Sandberg had Facebook cash-flow positive.

In early 2012, Facebook disclosed that its previous year profits had jumped 65 percent to $1 billion. Revenue, mainly from advertising, jumped almost 90 percent to $3.71 billion.

Facebook also reported that since 56 percent of its advertising revenue was from the United States, far more remained for harvest throughout the rest of the world.

With cash to invest, Facebook bought up many ancillary service providers. These included games, news aggregators, contact-importing companies, and photo-sharing services. Zuckerberg bought Instagram for a billion, and then scarfed up WhatsApp-a smartphone instant messaging application-for $19 billion more.

By the time January 2014 and Facebook's10th birthday had rolled around, the site had grown from a school-centric startup to a global behemoth and household name with a stunning, unmatched consumer data repository.

The company relentlessly tinkered with design and experimentation, with each successive data-mining design change aimed at gleaning deeper personal user insight. In addition to more user interaction features and additional functional capabilities, changes were also aimed at gaining one other important strategic advantage: keeping users on the site as long as possible.

The company remains determined to go wide-to blanket the planet-and also deep. The goal was, and remains, to accumulate as much personal data as possible to enable the success of its cash paying advertisers.

Summing up

When the recession hit, we plummeted from a good place to a bad place like an anvil down an elevator shaft. Most of the world plunged behind us. Jobs disappeared, debt choked millions, retirement plans were abandoned, and stress soared to dangerous and increasingly fatal levels.

Money was tight, so people stayed home and watched their televisions. They ventured out to see the world not by an expensive vacation, but rather a computer portal. The computer could take us anywhere, whenever we wanted to go.

And when we needed a new distraction, we got one: the smartphone. With it came easy outreaches, replies, and limitless touches with family and friends–*plus* a built-in camera to take pictures of *me* whenever I want. Best of all, those photographs didn't cost a dime to develop.

This was our world. Outside pressures caused a new austerity, and a steady stream of cost-effective digital friends arrived to serve all interests and help pass the time.

The behavioral hook was set. Little did we realize how quickly life would change.

Chapter 2

Where We Are

Workforce Demographics

Since the recession the workplace has changed swiftly and dramatically. In 2008 Millennials, those born between 1981-1997, had entered the workforce in minority numbers. Today, at 35 percent, they comprise the largest workforce demographic. This year marks the first that Post-Millennials (born 1998 and later) have gone on payrolls and their one percent will increase as Boomers keep retiring.

Gen Xers, born between 1965-1980, now represent 34 percent of the work force. Boomers, the post-World War II children born between 1946-1964 who comprised half the nation's workforce 20 years ago, have dropped to 29 percent and continue to shrink.

Why this generational shift matters

Coupled with society's growing digital permeation, understanding the implications of this demographic shift in conjunction with the recession is vitally important.

Millennials have not only increased their presence in the workforce to outnumber all other generations, they are smart. Better educated than their predecessors, Millennials use digital tools as part of daily living. Because digital life is the only life they have known and organic in nature, proficiency is innate. While they may lack wisdom supplied by applied lessons learned from experience, Millennials certainly know where to find whatever information they are looking for.

By contrast Boomers, who a generation ago comprised nearly half the workforce but now represent slightly more than one-fourth, have had to adapt to technology. Forced adaptation has required "acquired skill" learning.

Boomers were raised with paper and pen, bound hardback dictionaries, and landline telephones. As each new gadget is introduced for mainstream acceptance, a Boomer must learn how to use it. While this puts them at a technological disadvantage, Boomers have two thing Millennials do not-a frame of behavioral reference and a far broader range of social experience.

Gen Xers, to some degree, are technology straddlers. For someone born in the 1960s, computers were fundamentally simple devices and cell phones arrived later on the scene. For those born near the end of the Gen X cutoff year (1980), technology was much more prevalent so adaptation was generally quick.

These "frame of reference" variances are why workplace confusion sometimes reigns. Boomers cannot fathom a young person's face-first addiction to a phone. Younger workers are mystified how Boomers survive without digital velocity.

Global Employment

While a rebounding economy would seem to expand the working class in both numbers of employees and declining percentages of unemployment, only the first half of that assumption is true. Automation and technology suppress the blue-collar job market, so the unskilled-those who use bodies rather than minds to generate revenue-find erratic work at flat wages, with many of those jobs at increasing risk of technological obsolescence.

Cyclical exceptions such as the boom or bust housing construction market exist, but robotics and imported goods from lower cost nations threaten career opportunities.

Global unemployment continues to project a disturbing, increasing trend. When the recession hit in 2008, approximately 177 million workers were out of work, a figure that has climbed steadily. Today roughly 210 million workers are out of jobs, which represents a full percentage point increase.

Automation is expected to keep these figures climbing at a similar steady rate.

U. S. household income declines

Domestically the distribution of household income in the United States has become dramatically more unequal during the post-2008 economic recovery. Using 2008 as the saddle year between 2005 and 2011-a timeframe that covers the end of the U. S. economic run-up, crash, and slow recovery-median middle class household wealth plummeted 35 percent, from $106,591 to $68,839.

The income inequality gap is disturbingly widespread. Occurring in more than two out of every three metropolitan areas, the rich are getting exceedingly richer, the poor continue to struggle, and the middle class is getting shoved down.

For the rich, life is good. Sales of private ultra-luxury yachts were up 40 percent in 2015, luxury car sales rose 17 percent, and value of fine wine and high-end wristwatches rose five percent. But these are toys for the elite, not the masses-for whom such luxuries will never be part of daily living.

When money is tight people spend less. When spending slows (or stops), people stay in. When they stay in, they have time on their hands. When they have time on their hands they go on-line.

Technology is the free portal to everything, a mistress of vicarious access.

Why this matters

Workplace uncertainty, flat wages, increasing automation, doom-and-gloom projections-plus having to cut back due to tight money-combine to create relentless stress. Bad news is easy to find on the nightly news, on-line, and babbling from the mouths of politicians who seem more skilled at pontificating the obvious than creating positive change for hundreds of millions clamoring for help.

Because frustration limits fulfillment, changing behaviors are feeding more negative thoughts than positive.

Declining optimism

Declining optimism, coupled with low consumer confidence, has painted the picture for many that we are still in a recession. Statistically speaking the recession ended at the end of 2009. Macro issues like the increasing federal debt and micro issues like hikes in food prices have, to a large extent, have been accepted as part of the new normal.

A 2011 poll (two years after the recession ended) found that more than half of Americans thought the U. S. was still in it. While this could have been because both private and public levels of debt were at historic highs in the U.S. and many other countries, this blanket of negative perception serves to suppress the emotional health of the collective populace.

Only a few, the "one-percenters," are rolling in money. The rest feel far less optimistic about public service and servants, economic opportunity, job security, and accumulation of wealth. Attitudinally, more are resigned to accepting the status quo than being brightly optimistic.

Optimism vs. Pessimism

Emotional positioning is important due to the behavioral differences between optimism and pessimism. When pessimism is the prevailing mood, negative news is seen as validation and the will to proceed is diminished.

To an optimist, negative news is a temporary delay and the will to persevere continues.

Later, when we examine which particular behaviors technology is making us do more and less of, it is readily apparent that individual frustration greatly influences optimistic and pessimistic perspectives.

U. S. Employment & Wages

For three decades leading up to the crash, the United States job market was steady and robust. Roughly 20 million jobs were added during the decades of the 1970s, 1980s, and 1990s. Seven million more were added leading up to the 2008 recession, which resulted in a precipitous drop of nearly nine million and created a net decade-loss. It has been a slow crawl back, with millions of families unexpectedly forced to deal with no work and crushing debt loads.

Household deleveraging-achieved by paying off or defaulting on debts-was most pronounced in the United States. On the tail end of the worst of it, 2012, about two-thirds of debt reduction reflected defaults.

With money hard to come by, staying afloat and getting ahead has remained a very difficult challenge. Stress remains while optimism is suppressed.

Salary trajectories

In November 2015 employment analysts at CareerBuilder and Economic Modeling Specialists Intl. (EMSI), a partner company that provides employment data and analysis, released a list of industries showing the largest pay increases. There aren't many.

The study results were gleaned from nearly 100 national, state, and local employment resources. From

2005 to 2015, the national average growth rate for earnings across industries was 2.1 percent. The good news: While 2.1 percent is hardly inspiring, at least it illustrates a positive trend.

Here's the bad news: Since the statistical end of the recession in 2009 and the start of 2010's economic recovery, average earnings among wage-and-salary workers have decreased 0.1 percent.

Why this flat money trend matters

It is tough to recoup lost wealth if wages and salaries are flat and for the past five years they have been. Treadmill finance-where someone works hard but does not feel he or she is getting anywhere-creates job and life frustration. Unhappiness leads to disengagement, and when unhappy people care less, a more cynically negative "Can't because" attitude replaces an optimist's far more positive "How can we?"

When no wage increases are in sight and worker loyalty diminishes, job-hopping for more cash becomes increasingly common. This is a conundrum for employers, as turnover is expensive. Employers don't pay more because they don't have to, so workers jump for increases in pay. Job-hopping hurts tenure, performance, and workforce stability, but for younger workers especially, it is the quickest way to financial gain.

Wages in broad sectors: Losers & Winners

The CareerBuilder and EMSI findings reported that between 2010 and 2015, wages declined in eight of the 20 broad industry sectors. Here are some winners and losers:

Losers

Hit hardest was Health Care and Social Assistance, which declined 4.4 percent. The biggest reason for the drop was a dramatic 20 percent wage cut in Individual and Family Services.

The Government sector saw the second largest wage decline (-3.1%), primarily due to budget cuts and downsizing.

Other broad industry sectors experiencing declines in post-recession earnings include:

- Retail (-1.7%)

- Accommodations and Food Services (-1.4%).

- Administrative and Support (-2.3%).

- Waste Management and Remediation Services (-2.3%).

Why this matters

These broad sectors represent a huge chunk of American jobs. When massive people-centric employment industries are hit this hard-to the point of year-over-year compensation decline-it is a long, slow climb back up the pay scale. Millions of workers resign themselves to believing that what they are doing is a job, but nothing more. Psychologically, diminishing personal fulfillment leads to a very uninspiring place.

Winners

Several broad industry sectors saw significant wage increases since 2010, with many involving high-paying work. Two on the list include:

- Information (+13.9%);

- Finance and Insurance (+4.2%).

Information, finance, and insurance are totally tech dependent. Since wages increase significantly only in job niches of escalating demand, the competition for workers skilled in the tech space is obvious. This is (and will remain) a very strong growth sector.

The CareerBuilder and EMSI report explained the dramatic Information pay hike this way: "The Information sector not only had the most wage growth post-recession, but also since 2005 (20 percent).

"Among reasons for this surge in earnings is a big jump in Internet Publishing and Broadcasting and Web Search Portal jobs, which on average earn upwards of $220,000 in 2015."

So despite tens of millions of losers in the flat wage era, skilled technology knowledge works are reaping increasingly big money. Wage growth has occurred primarily in what is known as the STEM-related fields (science, technology, engineering, and math) and is likely to stay that way.

Technology's Morphing Direction and Purpose

Device customization & Apps

As noted earlier, technology manufacturers continue to create and aggressively sell smaller, personal, portable, and seemingly ubiquitous devices. Customers now own multiple units rather than just one, each filling different needs. The key to driving device demand is customization, which is now achieved largely through "Apps."

Since Apple's App Store is the industry standard, we will use Apple's consumer demand data to illustrate the power of app creation and adaptation. Independent developers create apps. If the app meets Apple's guidelines it can be added to the App Store. There it can be directly downloaded to iPhones, the iPod Touch, and iPads. Laptops and desktop computers can acquire the apps through iTunes.

When the App Store opened in July 2008, app creation was relatively complex and choices were few. Since then app development has become cheap, fast, and easy.

The day after the App Store was created, Apple released the iPhone 3G, which was preloaded with App Store support.

The appetite for apps proved voracious and it took just 30 months for the ten *billionth* app to be downloaded. Six months later the total had rocketed to 15 billion.

Today Apple's App Store houses more than 1.4 million third party apps. In June 2015, Apple announced the App Store had passed 100 billion downloads. Given that the world population is 7.4 billion, Apple's totals alone average more than 13 apps for every man, woman, and child on earth.

Apps are a huge business but not everyone gets rich. Mobile expert Tomi Ahonen estimates that mean revenue for developers is roughly $8,700 but some developers hit home runs. Pollen VC Insights estimates that this year 1,260 developers will make at least $1 million.

While roughly one-third of apps are free, Sinead Carew of Reuters points out the rest sell for an average of $3.64. A million dollars divided by $3.64 means a whole lot of people are paying a ton of cash for convenience. If you can fill a mass market need, there is money to be made.

Not surprisingly, the end of app growth is nowhere in sight. As many as 60,000 apps are added monthly. Thanks to their refined simplicity of invention, this growth rate is increasing too.

The app trendline points specifically toward the customer. Allow people to customize their device and they will do so. If they customize it, they will use it. Provide new reasons to use the phone and they will do that too. Americans spend more time on their phones than anyone-according to cell phone data tracker Informate Mobile Intelligence a daily average of 4 hours, 47 minutes-and apps are a big reason why. Phones have imploded the wristwatch, digital camera, and alarm clock industries. They have also cut into flashlight and battery sales, as well as photo processing.

Apps are spokes to expanded possibilities, with the phone as the hub. Mobile phones, in theory, were invented so people could talk. But phone calls are the sixth most used function. Greater utility is found with web browsing, app usage, texting, checking social media, and gaming.

App versatility and popularity is a big reason we see increasing numbers of people sitting, walking, and waiting with their heads down instead of up. When people care less about what is around them in deference to what is right in front of their noses, they are free to disappear inside a portal of customized distraction.

The old days of off-the-shelf, take-it-or-leave it product design work only for supporting peripherals. Everything else about the industry is catered toward increasing personal relevance. This is how the money is made and customer engagement is maximized.

Behavioral Impact of Post-recession Communication Changes

The behavioral shift from how we used to communicate to how we do today includes more than just devices. There are four elements of effective communication: the sender, receiver, channel, and message. The channel is the communication vehicle we use to deliver the message.

A quick stroll through changing channels of choice over time includes person-to-person voice, the written word, typed and printed documents, printed fax, digital (non-printed) word processing, digital fax, emails, texts, interactive phone, voice mail, and instant messaging. What's really on fire now is none of them; it is video and video is exploding.

Facebook, the social media kingpin, saw video posts quadruple in a single year. The catalyst? The well-known "ALS Ice Bucket Challenge." Everyone did it, and everyone became a star.

Not only did people immediately post more videos with increased frequency, how they chose to watch these videos changed too. Viewers went small. According to Pew Research, approximately 75 percent of videos are watched on mobile devices.

Millennials-the largest segment of the workforce-are a major reason why. Millennials average roughly 100 daily phone checks. Sixty percent visit Instagram-an online photo sharing and social networking site-an average of ten times per day.

For the majority of owners, phone loyalty extends way beyond use. The power of attraction, its lure of digital seduction, is measured best when we realize that 80 percent of people under the age of 30 who have a phone never turn it off. According to AT&T and Dr.

Dave Greenfield of the Center for Internet and Technology Addiction, 61 percent of Americans-regardless of age-sleep with their phones, while 53 percent get upset if without theirs. Dr. Greenfield even coined a term for phone separation anxiety: "nomophobia."

The U. S. cell phone market is heavily penetrated-77 percent of us own at least one-but the relentless avalanche of content flying to, though, and from them points out two key things:

1. No messages have staying power.

2. Everything evaporates.

Advertising & the Art of Influence

Proliferation

Network television advertising is largely regulated. The average half-hour sitcom is 23 minutes of show edited and spread among fourteen 30-second commercials. Advertisers must target a message to the expected audience and that message either lands or bounces. Repetitive ads for the same product might be annoying to the viewer, but the advertiser is gambling that pounding the message home helps it sink in.

Newspaper advertising is evaporating. Long the backbone of consumer selling, technology has neutered its effectiveness. Money traditionally poured here is now funneled into cyberspace because cyberspace advertising offers two big advantages, personalized targeting and no limits on frequency. The web offers limitless, unregulated ad space. Much like a rush hour train in Beijing, regardless how crowded it seems, there is always room for one more.

Legendary MIT computer scientist Joseph Weizenbaum, whose work examining the relationship between computer power and human reasoning led the digital world to artificial intelligence, saw the clutter coming.

Shortly before his death in 2008, Weizenbaum said, "The Internet is like one of those garbage dumps outside of Bombay. There are people, most unfortunately, crawling all over it, and maybe they can find a bit of aluminum, or perhaps something they can sell. But mainly it's garbage."

If Dr. W thought it was bad then, he should see it now. Ads follow user curiosity. Despite increasingly cluttered web pages, every time we jump from one to read an article of interest, we must wade through more ads. We tolerate annoying, unregulated pop-ups, force-watch video advertising, and absorb the intrusions.

Then we surf on. Rather than log off and escape the blizzard of ads, our average online engagement times continue to increase. This is great for advertisers, who do not care how much time we waste. They want eyeballs and money.

To frame advertising proliferation in modern context, lives lived by Boomers were quieter and far less noisy. Fifty years ago a person could expect to see one million ads in his or her lifetime.

Today? Today we are exposed to somewhere between one million and 1.3 million *per year*—as many as 100 million over the same length of life.

Targeted Spend

In the February 2015 issue of Entrepreneur magazine, digital ad trend expert Ted Dhanik shared insight on the future of "native ads."

"When websites feature advertisements that emulate the content and style of their own site, we consider it native advertising. Native ad spending will climb from $3.2 billion in 2014 to $8.8 billion by 2018, largely because advertisers are seeing above average engagement."

Dhanik explained the difference between native ads and traditional methods.

"Native ads are typically long-form blog posts, infographics or videos that aim to inform, entertain and inspire people without directly promoting a product.

"For example, a banner ad from a clothing retailer might promote a winter clothing sale, but a native ad from the same retailer might discuss winter fashion tips instead. Typically, native ads are tagged with a disclaimer such as "sponsored content", "paid post" or "promoted by".

The reason why is the target audience. Millennials don't like "salesy" ad content.

Dhanik also pointed out that publishers are now partnering with advertisers throughout the production process. By helping each other write and edit, collaboration makes it much easier to produce effective output.

Behavioral Data

New channels, tactics, and advertising payment models only work when persuasive messaging lands solidly on a target audience. Behavioral data has power; it lets advertisers target people and demographics who fit customer profiles. By cutting data multiple ways, advertisers can profile a group based on analyses of online searches, browsing patterns, and purchase histories.

Behavioral targeting is vitally important and often makes the difference between a bungled or ultra-successful campaign.

Digital advertising is also moving full speed ahead in three other areas:

1. Mobile video ads

2. Native advertising

3. Viewable impressions.

Also worth watching is the rapid evolution and mutation of the digital advertising industry. Delivery channels change, as do customer habits, interests, preferences, and decision-making processes. Ad strategies have shelf lives, and what worked in the past or works today will not work forever.

There is a huge push and increased spend in video ads, largely because production costs have plummeted. Amit Chowdhry summarized in Forbes the major moves kingpin players have made to invest heavily in the video arena:

- Yahoo! paid $640 million in cash for video advertising company BrightRoll, which processes 30 billion ad-related data points per day and specializes in campaign optimization.

- AOL bought Adap.tv for $405 million in cash and stock. At the time (August 2014) CEO Tim Armstrong said he was motivated by the trend away from linear TV to online video, plus the move toward programmatic media buying.

- Facebook bought LiveRail for between $400-and-$500 million. LiveRail enables publishers to push ad inventory across all devices and serves around seven billion ads per months.

- In 2014 Google bought mDialog privately, a company that lets publishers monetize video content.

- Also in 2014, Comcast bought FreeWheel for $375 million. FreeWheel works with web companies to deliver video ads.

Online time is increasing

The reason for the hefty investments is that people are spending more time on-line. Sources eMarketer and Leichtman Research Group (LRG) peg Millennials at 3.3 hours per day, Gen Xers at 2.8 hours per day, and Boomers at 2.1. These figures continue to grow steadily, and video is a great tool to help engagement times protract.

Consulting firm eMarketer also published a trend data summary report in January 2016 that is especially eye opening. Digital display ad revenue will, for the first time, surpass search ads. While both categories are exploding with double-digit year-over-year growth projected through 2019, the velocity of accelerated spend into the unregulated digital ad world is impressive.

The combined search and display revenues track like this:

- 2014: $44.51 billion.

- 2016: $61.41 billion.

- 2019 *(projected):* $87.29 billion.

With cost of creation decreasing and insight increasing, the five-year doubling of ad revenues portends an obvious future reality: *Advertising will proliferate to a width, depth, and sophistication way beyond anything we have ever seen.* Eyeballs will be bombarded.

Time choices

TV viewing minutes are up, time spent on-line is up, and cell phone engagement minutes are up. Logic dictates that the more digitally engaged we are, the less digitally un-engaged we must be.

Since everyone is awake the same finite amount of time each day-16 hours, assuming we sleep for eight, which I realize is a bogus assumption for many-it is worth examining how eyeball and keyboard time might affect other activities of life.

When teaching time utilization and time choice decision-making, I ask people to break their 16 daily waking hours into four categories:

1. Spent time

2. Wasted time

3. Invested time, and

4. Cherished time.

Efficient, happy, and productive people waste and spend as little as possible so they can maximize investment and cherish time. Investment time involves things of personal importance, often unrelated to money. Cherish time is special time, a very important ingredient for gratitude and happiness.

While it is easy these days to be busy, it is hard to be productive. The difference between the two is found in time-choice decision-making.

People who are frustrated or unfulfilled generally waste and spend too much time on activities that yield little or no return. The more time they spend and waste, the less remains for things that might yield a better payoff.

High performance happiness model

Mediocre performance model

The pie charts above show how highly efficient performers use their time more effectively than others. Day after day better choices add up; and over time they will create a tremendous difference in achievement, self-fulfillment, and contentment.

Shown below is a chart that illustrates various activities tied to each of the four time-use categories: Waste, Spend, Invest, and Cherish. These are subjective topics, so people may categorize things differently. The chart provides a feel for how some activities clearly yield greater emotional return than others.

Following the time choice example chart is a simple explanation of why we choose to do some things but not others, and how anyone motivated to make better time decisions can quickly learn to do so.

TIME CHOICE EXAMPLES			
WASTED TIME	**SPENT TIME**	**INVESTMENT TIME**	**CHERISH TIME**
Hangovers	Commuting	Personal time (an investment in self)	Kindness to strangers: being significant in the lives of others
Mindless Internet use & chronic Facebooking	Housecleaning	Quality sleep time (8 hours a night)	True family time
Unrecorded commercial TV	Yard work	Pursue interesting hobbies	Self-reflection
Excessive texting & digital addiction	Doing laundry	Social interaction activities	Gratitude awareness & being grateful

WASTED TIME	SPENT TIME	INVESTMENT TIME	CHERISH TIME
Endless selfies	Medical care and doctor's visits	Proactive career development & life planning	Pursuing and embracing moments of pure bliss when it occurs
Reruns (when you've already seen something multiple times)	Proper vet care for pets	Thank you cards and phone calls	Recognizing and archiving great memories as they occur
Talking head instigators (TV/radio)	Grooming	Reading	Charity work
Performing serial tasks that could be accomplished via job overlap	Dressing	Experiencing new people, places, things, and cultures	Helping those who are struggling
Traffic jams	Waiting	Proactive car maintenance	Giving back
Un-zoned travel (not utilizing a logical circle route)	Home repairs and maintenance	Getting out of your comfort zone	Looking through old photo albums, scrapbooks, and keepsake boxes
Stinkin' thinkin'	Paying bills	Understanding finances	Volunteering
Excessive worry about the wrong things	Dealing with your email box	Understanding your insurance coverages	Helping others feel valued and important

WASTED TIME	SPENT TIME	INVESTMENT TIME	CHERISH TIME
24/7 work access: never truly escaping	Researching options	Staying fit: physically & mentally	Being significant in the lives of others
Being mean	Light reading	Being nice	Coaching children
Being judgmental	De-cluttering	Spiritual renewal	Kind gestures to strangers
Robotic monotony (reflexive looping)	Polishing shoes	Getting organized and decluttered	Mentoring someone in need
Dealing with time wasters, both man and machine	Waiting in line or for someone	Budgeting and managing your money	Doing something that makes you feel like a kid
Handling papers multiple times	Dealing with customer service	Pursuing happiness	Visiting someone in the hospital
Hoarding	Buying groceries and staples	Networking with real humans	Private time during a cemetery visit

With digital ad spend cluttering our lives to an often inconvenient and steadily increasing degree, it may be worth considering different time choices that best suit the simplicity of life you prefer. Minimizing the number of ads you ingest and replacing that time with something that yields a better emotional payoff may help.

How to Make Better Time Choices: Think > Feel > Do

It is easier to decide to change a behavior than actually do it, so it helps to understand what causes behavior in the first place. Thoughts create feelings, but feelings drive what we do.

Feelings are emotional conclusions we reach after evaluating a collected series of thoughts. In order to reach an emotional conclusion strong enough to act upon, we must decide one of two things:

1. We are better off for doing it (a reward).

2. We can avoid something bad happening (a negative consequence).

When your head is in the right place-receptive to change for the right reasons-making better choices gets easier. Instead of thinking about doing things differently, you know what to do, why you are doing it, and feel confident taking action.

It is inarguable that technology permeation has radically influenced behavior, but the two-pronged fundamental principle behind human behavior remains constant and bears repeating:

1. *What we think shapes how we feel.*

2. *How we feel-the emotional conclusion(s) we reach as a result of accumulated thoughts-drives what we do.*

Accumulated thoughts, both positive and negative, continually reshape our outlook. While our life lens and core beliefs are established during our formative years of 0-to-13, reshaping continues due to good and bad significant emotion events, as well as life's steady stream of experiences.

Since technology enables a remarkably accelerated accumulation of thoughts, it is vital to understand the battleground between your ears. Technology use is the modern gateway to thought collection, which in turn shapes emotions and influences actions.

This rapid accumulation of horizontal and vertical thoughts-what we know, and what we know *that matters* (emotionally)-crowds brains in positive and negative ways. This percolating matrix of blended trivial and important thoughts shape the emotional conclusions that determine what we choose to do.

Thoughts shape positive *and* negative emotional conclusions, but fear is the dominant behavioral motivator-which is why the cesspool of national politics bubbles in toxic goo-so it is important to recognize that fear and doubt crowd the mind with negative emotional beliefs.

The challenge of maintaining a happy, well-balanced outlook in a technology-influenced society depends on minimizing negative emotion-creators and maximizing positive behavioral interactions.

Whether we are walking around thinking or sitting at a keyboard processing digitally influenced thoughts, once information percolates to the point of creating emotional conclusions strong enough to act upon, we act. But if all of those thoughts we collect create nothing more than an ambivalent emotion, we do nothing.

When we soon examine the specific behaviors technology is causing us to do more and less of, every one ties back to this powerful principle of human behavior. Each will be perceived as an aid toward a positive reward, or negatively as something connected to a potentially negative consequence.

Payoff & Priority

Once we own the importance of making smart time decisions, and understand what causes us to do or not do something, one of the best tricks to being less busy and more productive is to evaluate options two ways:

1. *Payoff.* Is the payoff large, medium, small, or microscopic?

2. *Priority.* Is the option urgent, important, unimportant, or a relative waste of time?

Since time is finite, and the goal is to work smarter, pick activities based upon what matters most and needs to be done first.

Time choices and happiness

Time choices are important to happiness because people who make continually good choices get more done than others; and productive days produce positive feelings of accomplishment. They also produce better results. People who are frustrated or unhappy typically are not pleased with how their time is passing by. There is a tremendous emotional gap between the endorphins of a great, productive day and the discouragement of a wasted one.

The Internet and smartphone are seductresses-both will coax you in-but lingering too long serves the toolmakers, not you. Be vigilant of how "toy time" passes. Smart time choices ensure that you are managing your tools and they are not managing you.

Mapping your current behaviors against desired time choices

It helps to map the emotional effects of increasing and decreasing behaviors against your desired state of positive time choices.

If your current time choices are not delivering what you want out of life, introspectively examine how time passes by. Do less of low return activities and more of things that matter.

But if you have a happy, fulfilling, high-performing life-protect it. Time wasters are everywhere. Some are machines, others are human.

Next we examine specific behaviors impacted by technology in two ways: things we are doing more of and things we do less frequently. Many will ring quite familiar.

What We Are Doing More & Less Of

The remarkable acceleration and increasing reliance and permeation of technology is radically changing human behavior in very recognizable ways.

Some of these changes are beneficial. Others are potentially dangerous physically and emotionally. Spurring on these behavioral changes, the ramifications of which too many millions underestimate and do not understand, are emerging technologies devised to entice greater engagement than older, familiar ones. At stake for product manufacturers are eight things:

1. *Huge sums of money*

2. *Market acceptance*

3. *User engagement and increased reliance*

4. *Market share*

5. *Strategic positioning*

6. *Related peripheral sales*

7. *Behavioral analytics*

8. *Advertising enablement.*

This section shares 21 specific examples of behaviors we now do more frequently, as well as 14 behaviors we do less often.

After sharing these changes, we will overlay them against time-use decision-making and examine the impact those changing behaviors are having on happiness.

We will also examine these changing behaviors from a second vitally important perspective: How they, along with the social media "Facebook Effect," map against Abraham Maslow's Hierarchy of Needs and the pursuit of personal fulfillment.

The results are startling.

Changing Behaviors: Things We Are Doing More Often

TABLE 1: THINGS WE ARE DOING *MORE* OF		
ASPECT	**DESCRIPTION**	**IMPLEMENTATION EXAMPLE**
Global engagement	Social, political, financial, religious, etc.	Understanding, misunderstanding, information and "misinformation" are all increasing.
Digital addiction, addiction denials, addictive behavioral justification	Alarming growth in this new area of study, the first where the afflicted have no desire to be cured, simply the desire to "manage it better."	Fatalities from texting and driving, rising injuries from texting while walking, death by video game marathons, etc.
Stress and fatigue	Technology is a silent partner, so the pressure to produce and get ahead or meet expectations builds.	People who are "busy" but not productive feel fatigue. Fatigue leads to negative behavioral choices.
Texting/dopamine craving	The pursuit of dopamine jolts is addictive.	Power and jolt of dopamine release depends on the importance of the sender.
Helicopter and digital parenting	Smothering choice-and-consequence learning through technological blanketing and meddling.	Feeding digital addiction via gadgetry to keep the child occupied, rather than behavioral accountability and emotional maturity.
Snap judgments	Instant info knee-jerks instant decision-making.	Management by fact supplanted by assumptive judgment.

Aspect	Description	Implementation Example
Reckless driving and road rage	Technologically driven impatience and desire for immediacy transfers to behaviors behind the wheel.	Diminished cognitive emotional control dramatically increases risk.
Telepressure	The feeling that we must be available 24/7.	Majority of Millennials never turn off (and sleep with) their phone.
Password insanity and the frustration that goes with it	Sites and organizations create rules for their convenience, not ours.	Accelerated confusion and frustration become a sustained hassle.
Oversubscription	The frenzied desire to cram more into each day.	Frustration that comes from mistaking relentless busy for efficient and productive.
Complication of things that require no complication	The extra decisions and steps and decisions now required to execute what used to be a menial task.	The multiple button-pushing selections now required to simply buy and pump petrol at the station.
Skyrocketing advertisements via abrupt, incessant, annoying intrusion	Ads on the Internet are limitless and unregulated; each designed to inspire a need or inadequacy.	Fifty years ago a person saw one million ads in a lifetime. It is currently over one million per year and rising.
"Busy" (the velocity of life)	The busier the person, the shorter the attention span.	Sedentary busyness contributes to physical and mental fatigue.
Increased speed of "3-headed"* cranial juggling	*How we *want* to appear to others, how we *do* appear to others, and *who we really are*.	Teen and college suicides increasing due to inability to reconcile negative perceptions of others.

ASPECT	DESCRIPTION	IMPLEMENTATION EXAMPLE
Portals into the mind	The more we invent to simplify our lives, the more complicated it becomes.	More access vehicles than ever, all designed to jam more thoughts into the mind.
"Do-it-yourself" society	An evolving behavioral exodus from service-centric interactions.	Often frustrating, time-consuming, and unrewarding.
Frustration and impatience	Technology is all about speed, access, and immediacy. None of these teach patience.	Human attention spans shortening. Recently measured akin to that of a goldfish.
Cyber-criminals, cyber-bullies, and the growing threat of cyber-terrorism	None of these existed a generation ago. Now they loom as inevitable foes.	Strike at the emotional core of safety and survival.
Instant notoriety (both good and bad)	People used to have to *accomplish* something to become noteworthy. Now they simply have to *do* something.	"If it bleeds, it leads." The media can make instant martyrs of anyone; or instant celebrities without regard to earned achievement.
Political cesspooling	"What is wrong with the other guy" has supplanted "What I stand for" in American politics.	Indefensible fear mongering sells and works better than facts and objectivity.
"Gotcha" political correctness	The web grabs misspoken statements faster and easier than a farmer traps a mouse in a grain silo.	What someone says too often taking back seat to what he or she truly means. With no defense or recourse.

Item by Item:

1. *Global engagement.* As unfathomable as it seems for a Millennial, 50 or so years ago Americans had their choice between three TV networks-ABC, CBS, and NBC-and all three stopped broadcasting at 11 PM. News came primarily from a daily newspaper. What Americans learned about distant lands arrived monthly to subscribers in a slick, glossy, photo-rich magazine called *National Geographic.*

   Digital technology did us a big favor, in that it lassoed the planet and tugged it tight. World awareness is up, communication is up, and global issues are solved for. Unfortunately, bad guys from all over now have a global sand box in which to play.

2. *Digital addiction, addiction denials, addictive behavioral justification.* Ten video gamers have died from pulmonary embolisms after playing non-stop marathon sessions that lasted between 12 hours and three straight days. It is common for young girls to text over 3,600 times per month while anxiously checking their phones for more. While girls text for social connection and boys to send information, girls are more likely to get hooked on compulsive behaviors, which statistically

correlate to lower grades in school. Researchers attribute the decline to the personal nature of chronic distractions.

Digital addiction clinics and treatment programs are growing, as is their customer base. The big danger with digital addiction isn't simply sheer numbers. Unlike other health-threatening addictions such as drugs, alcohol, and overeating, the digitally addicted have no desire to quit; they simply want to learn how to better manage their dependence. Digital addiction is a rapidly expanding worldwide menace.

3. *Stress and fatigue*. Digital immersion creates exhaust fumes in the brain and sedentary behavior morphs the physique. Eyestrain, fatigue, "'text neck" (a physical malady that comes from a bent head straining the neck muscles for long periods of time) and the emotional pings that come from prolonged vid screen engagements all sap energy. The head weighs 8-to-12 pounds. Bending the head forward 45 degrees, common for texters, creates 49 pounds of force. As engagement times increase, so does fatigue.

4. *Texting/Dopamine craving*. The appeal of texting is chemical. When we send and receive texts our brains release shots of dopamine, the body's version of cocaine. The more desirable the source

of the message, the greater the jolt. Text addictions come from the relentless pursuit of dopamine, our body's "happy drug." Silicon Valley knows this but The Valley doesn't care about feeding addictive behaviors. The Valley cares about revenue.

5. *Helicopter, digital, and lawnmower parenting.* The number of "smother mothers" (and fathers) using digital devices to quiet or preoccupy their children is rising. This is not unexpected. If you are raised knowing nothing but a digital world, extending that digital world to your offspring seems right and natural. And because parents *can* stay in touch, they do.

Boomers grew up in a time unencumbered by digital tethers. But today digitally-enabled helicopter parenting is a problem extending beyond grade school into and through college, even into the work force, where some parents meddle in their child's career. This digital cling is a trait of wired generation parenting that has grown from an anomaly to fairly common.

"Lawnmower parenting," where parents keep stepping in front of children to intercede, remove barriers, and clear the way, is more severe and also increasing, especially in colleges. Counselors stuck dealing with these relationships opine that no young adult will learn decision-making and accountability unless he or she is free to make decisions and own the consequences.

6. ***Snap judgments.*** Digital interactions create immediacy of engagement, expectation, and response. Technology feeds this with a relentless march of faster devices. Engaging with digital tools requires a series of progressive decisions. Impatience and assumptions trump in-depth understanding as the prevailing drivers of habitually quick decision-making.

7. ***Reckless driving and road rage.*** Because more people and cars are jammed onto existing roadways and outdated bridge infrastructures, traffic is worse than ever. Wait times keep increasing as rush hours lengthen and metropolitan traffic worsens. In a hurry-up world of increasing digital engagement, tight money frustrations, fatigue, and political anger creating schisms among ethnicities, it is not surprising that road rage cases continue to rise.

Road rage is a perceived violation of personal space, with the car an extension of self. Threats trigger an emotional choice to fight or flee. With guns in America as common as coloring books, unvented anger can escalate. Not all victims are motorists. In 2015, a 4-year-old girl in Albuquerque was shot and killed by an angry driver.

Road rage's stat trend is disturbing, the numbers even worse.

The American Automobile Association (AAA) started tracking and analyzing driver violence based upon 10,000 traffic accidents over a seven-year period that linked to more than 12,500 road rage injuries and 218 deaths, most of which were deliberate murders by angry drivers. Alarmingly, this number has been steadily increasing seven percent each year.

Aggressive driving causes roughly two-thirds of all accidents, with 37 percent of traffic fatalities stemming from trigger-fingers and firearms, not impact collisions.

If you find yourself suddenly involved in a scenario that alarms an emotional reaction-whether from racing, tailgating, someone failing to observe signs, ignoring regulations, or driving aggressively and seeking confrontations-do not take the bait.

Reactive survival instincts flood the mind with adrenaline-filled stress that stems from a very identifiable source. The other driver is intentionally violating your personal space. You have a choice to confront or avoid. Never confront, always avoid.

8. ***Telepressure.*** Telepressure is a fairly new, self-created but growing phenomenon whereby a person feels "obligated" to be digitally accessible at all times. The work justification is commitment and allegiance. The social need feeds on not wanting to miss out.

   Telepressure allows for no separation between work life and home life. Brains have a finite capacity to withstand this. Without true relaxation time to rest and recharge, sooner or later Humpty Dumpty shall fall.

9. ***Password insanity and the frustration that goes with it.*** The more we rely on our gizmos, the more sites we visit. The more sites we visit, the more engagements we have. The more engagements we have, the more we need to create and change an increasing number of passwords. Chaos reigns, of course, because invisible others determine creation rules and change governance. We are forced to react to their whims, which is inconvenient at best but frequently annoying. We must also keep track of them, which burns wasted time on non-productive activities that yield no payoff.

10. *Oversubscription.* The adage "If you want something done, give it to a busy person" sometimes bends the truth. Oversubscription refers to busy people who cram so much into their lives their sleep, happiness, and battery recharging downtime suffer, so personal effectiveness is compromised. Attention spans shorten, quality execution is compromised, mistakes and omissions rise, and burnout may eventually come calling.

11. *Complication of things that require no complication.* Purchased gasoline at the pump lately? If so, how many decisions did you have to make, how many buttons did you have to push? All you wanted was ten gallons of petrol. How hard can it be? *Quite,* apparently.

    Pay inside or outside? Debit or credit? Enter your zip code. Enter your telephone number or swipe your frequent customer card. Car wash, press Yes or No. Receipt or no receipt? Select grade and press Start.

    All we want is *gas.* The extra task complexity is enough to make a person scream.

12. *Skyrocketing advertisements via abrupt, incessant, annoying intrusion.* The Internet is a nonstop monsoon of advertising proliferation. Overall ad spend is increasing each year, all of it

going to digital. Ad intelligence is tracking every move we make. These are, unfortunately, the good old days. The bombardment will worsen.

13. *"Busy" (the velocity of life).* Increasing speed, heightened expectations, theoretical multi-tasking (a myth, by the way), and expected immediacy triggered by the pursuit of dopamine release combine to increase life velocity. As the growing number of people who feel anxiety when separated from their phones increases, so does the self-driven emotional need to be busy.

14. *Increased speed of "3-headed" cranial juggling.* The more deeply we disappear inside chronic texting and social media, the faster the heads shall toss. How we want to appear to others and how we do appear to others (validation or rejection) often supersedes the most important head of all, self-awareness.

15. *Portals into the mind.* Technology's smorgasbord of access enablers into the mind has never been greater. We've gone from landlines, newspapers, and network television to computers, laptops, tablets, and smartphones. Increasing numbers are on-line while watching television. Smartphone ownership has doubled in the past five years. Half of adults own tablets. Nearly 90 percent of adults

over the age of 18, and 90 percent of those living in households with earnings in excess of $75,000 annually, are smartphone owners. Computers are still popular, but purchases are dropping among adults under 30, who are opting more for cell and smartphones-which now, at 92 percent ownership-are America's most common digital devices.

The more access points there are into the mind, the easier the mind is to reach. Time is a byproduct of easy access, so engagement with devices protracts. The more unfiltered "stuff" pours into the mind, the more difficult the mountain becomes to sort and manage.

16. *"Do it yourself" society.* Book your own travel. Pump your own gas. Check yourself out at the store. Shop online more and go out less. As Walt Zimmerman, a longtime friend and business associate said one day over lunch, "It's not about the customer." We then swapped horror stories about shoddy customer service. Eric Brown, a commercial airline pilot who travels relentlessly, becomes absolutely unglued when he hears the words, "I'm sorry sir, there's nothing more I can do." With increasing frequency we are forced to deal with a lack of satisfactory human resolution.

Customer service seems up to us, which is frustrating because *we* are the customers.

17. ***Frustration and impatience.*** Technology's relentlessly increasing velocity fuels expectations of immediacy. Spokes of stress from myriad starting points collect in our minds. When dissatisfaction occurs, decorum goes out the window. Quicker than ever impatient people vent, often rudely. Twitter, which was developed to feed horizontal message distribution and rapid exchange, is known as a "hater's arena" for a good reason. *Scientific American's* Victoria Stern reported that 46 percent of users tweet frequently to vent anger. Thirty-seven percent of haters hope the person or target will read their rant.

Impatience is increasing swiftly. For example, as popular as video has become, 50 percent of Millennials will abandon a video that does not start within ten seconds.

18. ***Cyber-criminals, cyber-bullies, and the growing threat of cyber-terrorism.*** Bad guys love the Internet, which provides faceless power and ample opportunity for easy money. Hacking is a very lucrative profession. Bullying is a gutless but increasingly popular hobby, a new form of darkness now part of daily life.

19. ***Instant notoriety (both good and bad).*** Good news travels fast. Bad news travels faster. Want to get famous in a hurry? Post a sex tape or take money from your dental practice and shoot a beloved lion on an African game preserve.

20. ***Political cesspooling.*** This has devolved to the point of head-shaking disbelief.

21. ***"Gotcha" political correctness.*** The almost fanatical social obsession with how people want to appear to others drives the reflexive rock throwing of hypersensitive and sometimes self-righteous image-seekers. At the astounding rate digital dog piles continue growing, soon every opinion and punch line will require an asterisk and disclaimer.

Increasing Behaviors Summary

Reviewing the Increasing Behavior list clearly illustrates that many create negative emotional experiences, clearly to our detriment. Because these negatives add up, they can lead create pessimism, anger, and frustration. Negative emotions must then be offset by positive emotional experiences gained elsewhere simply to regain an even-keeled perspective.

Why this is potentially dangerous

When behavioral changes create negative emotional experiences, getting back to a positive place becomes a challenge. In order to reach a positive frame of mind, negative thoughts must be offset by experiential positives, be they from micro-moments or other interactions. Doing so often requires enhanced awareness, mind management, and conscious effort.

In a digital world, finding offsetting positives can become quite a tricky challenge.

Changing Behaviors: Things We Are Doing Less Frequently

TABLE 2: THINGS WE ARE DOING *LESS* OF

ASPECT	DESCRIPTION	IMPLEMENTATION EXAMPLE
Sleep	Quality, quantity, and REM are all negatively impacted by minds saturated by technological overcrowding.	Sufficient sleep resets the brain to allow us to wake refreshed and "ready to go" at the start of a new day. On March 1, 2016 a Nashville teenager, angered at being woken to go school, shot his grandmother, sister, and nephew.
Self-awareness	People are less cognizant of those around them, and the impact their behaviors may have on themselves and others.	Ten percent of all pedestrian visitors to hospital emergency rooms are caused by texting and walking.
Attention spans	Ability to concentrate noticeably diminishing.	Transient attention span now measured at eight seconds.
Fitness (physical and emotional)	Obesity and sedentary habits cause physical and mental challenges.	Strong of mind and body getting harder to find. Both require work, not shortcuts.
Manners	Self-preoccupation and a "me first" impulsiveness.	The downside of helicopter parenting: selfishness.

ASPECT	DESCRIPTION	IMPLEMENTATION EXAMPLE
Business maturity	Coddled students struggling to adapt to competitive landscape of workplace reality.	Job-hopping is rampant among the young. Companies scared to invest in workers; workers scared to invest in companies.
Wisdom	Knowledge is in the box now, not the mind.	*"You don't need to know anything any more. You just gotta know where to find it."* – American billionaire Mark Cuban, a tech mogul and star of TV's *Shark Tank*.
Patience	We are becoming more of an interruptive society that judges first, rather than seeking to understand.	Patience sports: hunting, fishing, sailing, golfing (for example) are all seeing markedly lower participation rates.
Ability to effectively manage the crowded mind's Worry Circle	Emotional illness worse now than during the worst of the recession. Crowded heads are not balanced heads. The ability to manage increased stress appears to be worsening.	Suicide rates in the USA have increased nearly 20 percent in the past 12 years. It is especially disturbing to note the rise in depression and suicide among the younger generation (mid-20s on down).
Critical thinking	People seek reaffirming evidence, rather than contrary.	Info is everywhere; but finding and objectively analyzing facts is becoming a lost art.
Privacy	None of us has privacy.	Personal intrusion—known or secret—exists for all.

Aspect	Description	Implementation Example
Accountability	Spin doctors, denials, PR firms, lawyers, and computer keystrokes deflect all.	Children reared without it become adults reluctant or unwilling to accept it.
Communication skills	Handwriting, grammar, spelling, and punctuation are the endangered rhinos of language.	Scores in core skills decreasing. Some USA schools replacing cursive handwriting with keyboard skills.
Feeling of productive, happy daily achievement	Technological immersion seems less an enabler than it possibly could be.	Just 30 percent of American employees feel engaged or inspired at their job, with 70 percent feeling unfulfilled.

Item by Item:

1. *Sleep.* Fried and frazzled minds require sufficient rest to reset. In simple terms, throughout the day the brain fires, burning energy that leaves debris on its floor. The debris needs to be swept out and the brain reset in order to wake fully refreshed. Sleep does this. A different part of the brain activates and provides this vital janitorial service.

   Generally speaking, it takes eight hours to do a thorough job. The reason we feel noticeably better after a good night's sleep than we do after short rest is that our mind is clear, cleaned and reset, and ready to go.

On short sleep the cleanup is halted before completion. We begin those days with leftover debris still remaining on an unclean floor and throughout the day we burn more energy and pile another day's debris on top of what was already there.

Despite sleep's importance, study trends indicate we are getting less of both REM and stage-four deep sleep. Some Fitbit-type gadgets try to measure this. Data is nice but gizmos really aren't needed. You know better than a bracelet whether or not you had a great night's rest.

From a physical standpoint, inadequate sleep contributes to weight gain, high blood pressure, depression, and lowered immunity. Domestically, the National Sleep Foundation reports that two-thirds of women have regular sleep problems and are susceptible to those maladies.

The Statistic Brain Research Institute reports that 40 percent of all Americans have a sleep disorder, with nearly two-thirds having a problem a few nights each week. Seventy million suffer from insomnia, with 20 million more dealing with restless leg syndrome.

Adults are recommended to get eight hours of sleep per night but three in 10 get less than six.

Teens need nine hours. Seven of 10 get less, and one-fourth are so fatigued they struggle to concentrate. Two separate studies shared in the Journal of Psychosomatic Research tie a direct relationship between loss of sleep and negativity. Babies are cranky when they need their rest. As it turns out, so are adults.

On insufficient rest, predictable things happen. One-third of Americans fall asleep during the day at least once a month, while one in 20 nods off while driving. Forty thousand car crashes occur annually from drivers falling asleep and fatalities-where the driver never wakes up-exceed 1,500 each year.

These sobering stats underscore why the doubling of energy drink sales since 2010 cannot counteract fatigue. Global research firm Mintel reported that older Millennials (27-to-37) are steadily increasing their use of energy drinks despite growing concern about the safety of ingredients. Sixty-one percent consume energy drinks currently, up 10 percent since 2014.

Sleep trends are bad in America but even worse globally. The World Association of Sleep Medicine reports that sleep deprivation negatively affects the quality of life for 45 percent of the world's population. It is tough for anyone to perform at peak potential when the person must drag himself or herself out of bed.

2. ***Self-awareness***. Oblivious texters walk off piers, fall into mall fountains, bang into streetlamps, and limp into emergency rooms. Google "texting accidents funny" and 36,600 clips come up. Some are quite entertaining.

   Concussions, broken legs, feet, and ankles-all result from talking and texting while walking. Injuries have multiplied *ten-fold* in the past decade, despite an overall decline in pedestrian visits to emergency rooms. Injury statistics indicate increasing numbers of people, especially those under 30, are lost in their phones and injuring themselves.

3. ***Attention spans***. *'Attention span'* is the measured amount of concentrated time on a task without becoming distracted. Joshua Conran recently wrote a piece for Inc.com about this, explaining that in today's click-skim-and-jump digital world, advertising and sales hooking efforts ultimately boil down to the first five seconds.

   This, he explained, is how quickly consumers decide whether they will buy into a brand or check out completely. This conclusion was reached based on research that concluded what many of us have been suspecting: Attention spans are rapidly dwindling.

In "Not Quite the Average: An Empirical Study of Web Use," a report written by the University of Hamburg's Harald Weinrich, Hartmut Obendorf, and Matthias Meyer in conjunction with Eelco Herder, data reveals that the average human attention span has plummeted to eight seconds-a precipitous drop from 12 seconds in 2000. If you have an aquarium at home, share the news with your goldfish. Goldfish have attention spans of nine seconds, so they are now more attentive than the average web-browsing human.

It is safe to assume that as digital reliance continues to strengthen, attention spans will further shorten. Other attention span stats of note include:

— Average number of times per hour an office worker checks his or her email: 30.

— Percent of page views that last less than four seconds: 17 percent.

— Percent of page views that last more than 10 minutes: 4 percent.

— Amount read on an average web page (593 words): 28 percent (166 words).

— Amount read on a web page with 111 words or less: 49 percent. This equals 54 words, one-third as many as the page with five times more content and the equivalent of two Tweets. People skim more than read.

4. *Fitness (physical and emotional).* Stress is up, digital addiction is up, traffic is up, income is stagnant, user time tied to digital engagement-a sedentary pursuit-is up. Fitness is struggling to keep pace.

The Physical Activity Council tracks American sports, fitness, and recreation participation in 120 disciplines. Their annual study for 2015 reveals that over the past few years, participation seems to be fluctuating but increases are seen in racquet, team, and water sports. Outdoor sports declined slightly while fitness sports remain flat. Although inactivity rose, those who are active seem to be participating more often and in multiple activities.

Most disconcerting are the overall levels of inactivity. Inactivity grew marginally in the last 12 months from 27.6 percent of Americans age 6+ to 28.3 percent. Only half of parents paid extra for their children to have fitness-related sports or exercise activities at school. Half chose not to.

Inactivity for the younger age groups flattened out in 2014, while there was a sharp increases of inactivity for those 65 and older. Ages 18-to-24 (Millenniums) show the biggest decrease, dropping 0.2 percent from 2013. Millenniums, of course, are the most wired generation.

The key takeaway is that inactivity seemed to increase among most ages, continuing a post-recession trend. There are 292 million Americans age 6 and older but 83 million are inactive, the highest rate in the past six years.

With the economy bouncing back and extreme weather conditions an occasional factor, Americans continue to struggle with physical activity commitment. Increasing numbers of people are making time use decisions unrelated to physical activity.

5. *Manners*. It is difficult to expect people oblivious to their surrounding to demonstrate a kind and considerate decorum. People text at church, the movies, concerts, and Broadway theaters. They know texting while driving a car is dangerous-distracted driving is roughly akin to three times the legal drunk-driving limit-yet still do it. When you drive behind a texter, it is obvious and frustrating. When you are waiting for a turn signal and get it,

but the car in front does not move, frustration grows. When people walk with their heads down and force you to step aside to avoid a collision, it is annoying. Living in oblivion is a personal choice with social ramifications.

6. ***Business maturity***. Coddled children raised with digital distractions who are used to instant gratification and participation trophies do not adapt as easily to the competitive world of business as those raised with higher expectations. One of the big vetting challenges for hiring organizations is figuring out which Millennium candidates have business maturity and which do not. This is a big frustration, because bad hires are expensive. Worker replacement costs typically range between 6X and 18X monthly pay, depending on the nature of the job. It is important to note that it is grossly unfair to pile on Millenniums as the only ones who cause such drama. Workers from all generations are culpable. Gen Xers can be frustrated easily by lack of upward mobility and flat wages and Boomers can be hanging on for the check rather than the work. A major part of business maturity involves the ability to work with concentration and discipline toward a time-sensitive business goal that relies on quality output. People with addiction and distraction problems, regardless of their generation,

contribute to a noticeable decline in workplace maturity.

7. ***Wisdom.*** Wisdom is the astute application of insight gained from experience. While Millennials are the smartest, best-educated segment ever to enter the American workforce, situational wisdom is not found on-line. People typically look up two levels for wisdom. For Millennials that means Boomers. With Boomers now exiting the workforce, that second generation source of wisdom and mentoring is dwindling for tech savvy Millenniums who have knowledge but lack experience and perspective.

8. ***Patience.*** Digital addiction feeds off of dopamine release and dopamine is most enjoyed in fast and frequent doses. As we have seen with attention spans, patience is being traded for expected immediacy. When a web page is slow to load, people jump. When we don't get what we want, we immediately look elsewhere. This craving for immediacy and action is one reason casinos proliferate while horse racing is dying. Slot machines, which are programmed to pay out only a percentage of what is wagered, have been so sped up by technology that players can now complete between 600 and 1,200 spins per hour. Las Vegas

machines are required by law to pay out at least 75 percent of what is wagered, although many casinos pay more than 90. Canada's rates are roughly 85 percent. Players don't care. Players like action, and 10 or 20 decisions per minute is a whole lot of action.

Horse racing, steeped in tradition and formerly the most popular spectator sport in America, is an industry that depends on pari-mutuel wagering. Racing in America dates back to 1665, and more than a century ago, in the mid-1880s, 314 tracks served an eastern-centric population of 55.9 million people.

Today roughly 75 horse tracks sell to a coast-to-coast nation of 320 million. Tracks are struggling because a two-minute race takes a half-hour to prepare for and run. By comparison, in that same half-hour, a slots player can experience 27,000 win/lose outcomes. Because players want decisions and are increasingly impatient to wait, the racing industry continues to lose customers.

9. *Ability to effectively manage the crowded mind's Worry Circle.* We will cover the Worry Circle in greater detail later in the book but basically speaking the Worry Circle is the imaginary bubble in the mind that houses everything we

worry about. With more portals (access points) into the mind and more information than ever flooding through our ears and eyes, Worry Circles can overload quickly. Stressed out people get that way because their Worry Circles have accumulated too many of the wrong things and they lack the life skills to manage the number down.

Hurting heads make rash emotional decisions. Emotion-driven stress is susceptible to volatile amplitude, often plummeting the distraught to very dark places.

10. *Critical thinking.* Critical thinking involves managing by fact and studying options from all angles prior to reaching a measured and fact-based conclusion. It is the antithesis of snap judgments. Immediacy, and the clamoring for immediacy, leads to snap judgments. Critical thinking is a powerful skill that involves cranial exercise and skilled thinkers do this well. Advancements in artificial intelligence are angling to replicate thought processes of the brain. If humans can't do it, smart machines will.

11. *Privacy.* Dr. Laura Schlessinger wrote something recently I enjoyed reading: "Remember when people had diaries and got mad when someone read them? Now they put everything online and get

mad when people don't." Privacy is a steamrolled, pancake-flat casualty of digital life. The government knows what you're doing, Internet cookies know what you're doing, and Facebook and its advertisers know your habits better than you. Lives of quiet, anonymous privacy are dodo birds. They do not exist.

12. *Accountability.* Want to guess who is responsible for fielding customer service calls for United Airlines? If you answered "Nobody," you are correct. When we fruitlessly navigate a website in search of a human contact phone number that does not exist, or wait like cattle between the ropes and finally reach a service agent, we gnash our teeth the moment we hear the dreaded words, "The computer says..."

The more people disappear inside computers, the easier computers are to hide behind. As customers, we have all dealt with the frustration of unaccountable behaviors. Automation keeps stripping the human element out of interpersonal contact and nothing joyful comes from mechanical interactions. Call centers formerly located in Bangalore that Americans vociferously complained about have, in many cases, been replaced by computers with voice recognition software that announce wait times. The company thinks this is good, but every customer stuck on hold wonders why a service rep's time is more valuable than his or hers. Negative emotions result, as no one likes being disrespected by unaccountable machines or companies.

13. ***Communication skills***. Technology has savagely butchered command of the language to the extent that there are now post-college training programs to close skill gaps in order for graduates to be able to communicate acceptably in competitive professional environments. Critically acclaimed linguist John McWhorter is an expert on the topic. McWhorter accepts that all languages mutate to some degree, but in his book *Doing Our Own Thing*, McWhorter reveals how cultural change is brutalizing the English language. "Street English," as he calls it, "is creating a great divide between written English and spoken English."

McWhorter makes no bones about the ramifications of where be believes we are headed and writes, "Our increasing alienation from "written language" signals a gutting of our intellectual powers, our self-regard as a nation, and thus our very substance as a people." A strong opinion, certainly, but few will debate that the digital world is dumbing down the command of basic, fundamental skills such as spelling, sentence structure, punctuation, and grammar.

14. *Feeling of productive, happy daily achievement.* A desk driver whose butt is parked in a chair all morning and afternoon and whose eyeballs are lost in a screen for hours on end does not leave at the of the day with a bounce in the stride or song in the heart.

Decreasing Behaviors Summary

Just as Table 1 previously showed how increases in certain behaviors negatively impact the mind, we add to that Table 2's list of Decreasing Behaviors. These changes impact all age groups, most dramatically the younger workers for whom technology and tool use is organic by nature. These behavioral changes are more obvious to those whose technological skills are acquired, as they must be for older workers raised in a pre-technology world. Older workers have reference points; they have a behavioral archive of these "before-and-after" life experiences and feel these changes firsthand.

Younger workers, for whom digital life is their only known norm, are usually oblivious to the impact of changing behaviors on their happiness and wellbeing.

Because they do not know any better, many lack the coping skills to recognize what is going on emotionally in order to self-correct.

Maslow & the 3-Headed Man

One of the founders of humanistic psychology, Abraham Maslow (1908-1970) was quoted describing the motivations behind his work in a PBS (Public Broadcasting System) sketch biography by saying, "I was awfully curious to find out why I didn't go insane."

The eldest of seven children, the Brooklyn native was smart but quiet, with an upbringing he described as somewhat lonely and unhappy. After attending City College in New York, Maslow preferred psychology to his father's preference for a law degree and left New York to study at the University of Wisconsin. He married his cousin and pursued an original and somewhat fitting line of research: primate dominance behavior and sexuality, a field he would continue researching at Columbia University.

From 1937 through World War II until 1951, Maslow was on the Brooklyn College faculty. He latched onto a pair of intellects whose work he found quite interesting, anthropologist Ruth Benedict and Gestalt psychologist Max Wertheimer. Both were tremendously accomplished in their fields and became trusted mentors and friends. They also piqued his curiosity.

Maslow studied their behavior and took copious notes, which provided true north for his research and thinking as they related to health and human potential. He wrote extensively, deep into the subject, borrowing and building on ideas from other psychologists. He zeroed in on concepts of a hierarchy of needs, metaneeds, self-actualizing persons, and peak experiences.

His body of work, new in its field, led to Maslow being embraced as a thought leader who explained life beyond Freud and behaviorism, the time's prevailing theory that assumed learners are passive and respond to negative and positive environmental stimuli.

Maslow believed there was more to life's progression toward happiness and fulfillment than simply reacting to rewards or punishment. He perceived human needs similar to a ladder with five progressive steps.

The most basic needs were physical survival necessities like air, water, food, and shelter. Then came safety and comfort, followed by psychological and social needs like belonging, love, and acceptance. Once those were met, he theorized people sought respect.

On his top rung were self-actualizing needs, which Maslow defined as the need to fulfill oneself by becoming everything he or she is capable of becoming.

Maslow felt that because the five steps were sequential, unfulfilled needs lower on the ladder were barriers. Individuals who made it to the top were what Maslow called "self-actualizing" people. Maslow's mentors, Benedict and Wertheimer, were his models.

Self-actualization included what Maslow defined as profound moments of positive emotional things. He described that place in life as, "When a person feels more whole, more alive, self-sufficient and yet a part of the world, more aware of truth, justice, harmony, goodness, and so on. Self-actualizing people have many such peak experiences."

While this explanation seems simple and logical now, Maslow's work at the time was perceived as radically different. His psychology peer group was not focused on studying happiness. Their worlds dealt with ill people and abnormal behaviors. The pursuit of happiness was his domain, not theirs.

Maslow's gift to future generations germinated from his quiet determination to pursue what mattered most to him. In that regard, he was self-actualized. Maslow wanted to unlock some secrets to positive mental health. He did, and all of us should be grateful he chose to study happiness instead of law.

When you look at his hierarchy chart below, note that the pursuit of happiness toward self-fulfillment starts from the ground up. The steps begin with Level 1, which is Safety. Once we are safe, we strive to reach Level 2, Comfort. Once we are comfortable we seek Level 3, Love and Affection. Once we experience emotional warmth, we seek Level 4, Respect.

Once we have respect, we are free to chase Level 5, Maslow's "Self-actualization." Here a person is doing what he or she was born to do. Cynics say Level 5 is unattainable. Behaviorists say, "Phooey! A fulfilling life is quite attainable."

Understanding this stair-step to happiness and fulfillment is important because all five levels tie directly to various changing behaviors caused by technology's influence. Having identified specific behaviors in life we are doing more and less frequently, we will now map them for better and worse against Maslow's Hierarchy of Needs.

The findings are unsettling.

Maslow's Hierarchy of Needs & 3-Headed Juggling

(note: The levels are listed from life's fundamental basics to the pinnacle of fulfillment.)

Level #, Maslow's Definition, and Comments

- *Level 1: Safety.* Examples include the European and Middle Eastern refugee crises. People are scrambling to simply find a place—any place—to carve out a life. Survival instincts in optimistic people are strong. Pessimists often surrender.

- *Level 2: Comfort.* Once we are safe, we seek comfortable surroundings. Worry Circle advice if you are comfortable: "Be grateful for what you have and worry less about what you don't." Gratitude calms a crowded mind. "Keeping up with the Joneses" does not define comfort. There is a difference between accumulating "stuff" and having what is needed, as needs and wants are different things. Comfort comes from having what you need.

- *Level 3: Acceptance, Love & Belonging.* People are herd animals. We seek love and affection, as well as acceptance by others. *Remember:* "Until you are happy with who you are, you will never be happy with what you have." Well-balanced people, those aligned between head and heart, have much to offer. Those who give love, affection, and support will find all three. Those devoid of caring for others risk isolation and loneliness.

- *Level 4: Respect.* Once we have acceptance, love, and affection, we seek the respect of others. This often requires adept awareness and skill for 3-headed juggling. Respect is granted based upon an emotional conclusion reached by others. The gang culture relies on this, because the gang fills respect-based emotional voids in members' lives. Status symbols project an image but not respect. The quickest way to gain respect is to give it.

- *Level 5: Self-actualization.* The ultimate pursuit. Doing what you were born to do. Tough to reach without smart, effective Worry Circle management, self-actualized people tend to have a great command of their true selves, warts and all.

Mapping Decreasing Behaviors Against Maslow's Hierarchy of Needs

When we map our previous list of 14 Decreasing Behaviors against Maslow's Hierarchy of Needs, we clearly see what is threatened. This chart starts with life's basics and progressively deepens toward the pursuit of happiness.

Decreasing Behaviors vs. Maslow's Hierarchy of Needs

MASLOW'S FIVE LEVELS	ASSOCIATED DECREASING BEHAVIORS
#1. SAFETY	• Privacy
#2. COMFORT	• Sleep (quality, quantity, and REM) • Ability to effectively manage the crowded mind's Worry Circle • Fitness (physical and emotional)
#3. ACCEPTANCE, LOVE, AND BELONGING	• Patience
#4. RESPECT	• Self-awareness • Attention spans • Manners • Communication skills: handwriting, grammar, spelling, punctuation, etc. • Business maturity • Critical thinking (managing by fact) • Accountability
#5. SELF-ACTUALIZATION	• Wisdom • Feeling of productive, happy daily achievement • Deep uninterrupted, reflective thought

Important: *Seven of the 14 decreasing behaviors negatively impact personal respect. Social ills like cyber-bullying, self-image and self-esteem problems, behavioral rancor, and gang influence all tie back to a natural human desire for Maslow's Level 4: Respect.*

The Maslow/Facebook Correlation

As Facebook has so remarkably demonstrated with 1.4 billion users communicating in 70 languages and participation rising 12 percent year-over-year, the global need to feed and replenish feelings diminished by the previously discussed changing behaviors seems insatiable.

With three-fourths of Facebook users living outside the United States, the emotional needs the site purports to fill are globally relevant. Nearly half of all users log in daily and spend nearly 20 minutes online, for a simple reason: They seek affirmations and reaffirmations throughout the course of daily living.

To underscore the impact of technology as it relates to both Facebook and Maslow's Hierarchy, it is vital to note that *eight* of our 14 identified Decreasing Behaviors (Levels 3 and 4) fall directly into the emotional gap-filling appeal of Facebook's wheelhouse. Additionally, the number one reason Facebooking creates negative emotional experiences for a large percentage of users is envy, which ties to Maslow's level four Respect.

The Envy Factor

When people read the posts of others and trigger the envy emotion, they are susceptible to increasing pangs of depression.

Passive engagement-where the user browses and reads but does not actively post or engage-typically creates envious thoughts. Active engagement-posting and commenting-does not.

The Facebook Effect, therefore, is largely up to us. People who compare themselves with others or feel jealousy easily should limit their use of social media. For people who are lonely and want to remain engaged, the key is remaining mindful of their vulnerability to negative thoughts. They will be better off actively engaging.

Forward-thinking society-shapers, such as researchers at M. I. T. working with futurist Dr. Agnis Stibe, are well aware of the Facebook Effect as they plan future city design. These technology-shaped communities will strive to maximize positive interaction, which will offset technology's normal negative impact on Maslow's two key levels, Level 3 (*Acceptance, Love, and Belonging*) and Level 4 (*Respect*).

The challenges and opportunities are right there for "think tanks" like M. I. T. to expand research and solve for. Whether they are designing a community of the future, shaping behaviors within that community, or simply innovating ideas on better ways for people to feel better about themselves while using technology, each creative stakeholder is empowered to be significant in the lives of others-an objective we all should embrace.

Selfies and Narcissism

Selfies are self-image and self-esteem boosts, and constitute a big part of social media popularity, an industry that leans heavily on image projection. Selfies comprise 30 percent of all photographs taken by people between 18 and 24.

Since 2012, the world "selfie" had grown in popularity by more than 17,000 percent. Half of men and women have taken them, and estimates on just how many we take range up to a trillion per year. Roughly 1.8 billion are posted online daily. Virtually none were taken in 2008 when the recession began.

Death By Selfie: 2015 Worldwide

Death by selfie is a new way to go. While sharks have been around for 420 million years and evolved into ocean denizens that kill each other and sometimes people, they never kill themselves. Eight humans died from shark bites during the same 12 months that 49 people met their demise saying "CHEESE!"

Zachary Crockett of Pricenomics compiled a list of 2015's selfie-related human fatalities. Not included is the death in Brazil of a rare baby porpoise, which was grabbed from shallow water near the beach, passed around a large crowd of beachgoers for endless selfies, and died of exposure.

Method & Number of Fatalities

- **Fall from heights:** 16

- **Drowning:** 14

- **Train accident:** 8

- **Gunshot:** 4

- **Grenade:** 2

- **Plane Crash:** 2

- **Car Crash:** 2

- **Animal:** 1* *(*a bull at Pamplona)*

Narcissism

A narcissist, by definition, is a man or woman who is vain, self-absorbed, and selfish. Narcissists take for their greatness for granted and are wired to believe they are better than all except their superstar peers. Because a narcissist assumes and truly believes superiority, he or she will be remarkably sensitive to criticism.

While narcissists love themselves, excessive selfies are not always proof that the person taking them is one. The vast majority of selfie-takers who post on social media are not narcissistic. What he or she seeks is affirmation from others.

If you have a relationship that causes you to think you may be dealing with a narcissist, visit *www.personality-testing.info* and take the quiz.

Why this matters

For much of the world the Internet is free. It is not a happy place. Bullies abound, takers will take, and haters will hate. But the fact that 1.8 billion photos are uploaded each day begs the question, "Why?"

As the world steadily becomes increasingly wired and people join social media looking for respect and acceptance to their best-projected self, it helps to understand the causes of emotional fragility and what we can do to help encourage happiness. Our understanding of the impact of changing behaviors on the human psyche is becoming increasingly important.

Concluding with the Maslow/Facebook Correlation

Facebook has remarkable numbers around the world for much the same reason: Through words and photos users seek Maslow's third and fourth levels, Acceptance and Love, plus Respect, during the normal course of daily living.

To underscore the impact of technology as it relates to both Facebook and Maslow's Hierarchy, remember that more than half of Table 2's fourteen Decreasing Behaviors (8 of 14) fall directly into the appeal of Facebook's wheelhouse, which revolves around self-image and self-esteem.

3-headed juggling

People are in different places experientially, as well as different places emotionally, so it helps to understand motivational priorities.

A person's behavioral choices will change only after he or she decides to change them, and change decisions will be acted upon only when the contemplated change is congruent with what someone feels is necessary.

What matters *most* depends upon how that person sees him or herself relative to their three-headed hydra of self-image, self-esteem, and self-awareness. Each of us has, and juggles, these three heads throughout our lives.

Since our three-heads are sometimes moody, behaviors depend upon how loudly each head clamors for attention.

The heads are:

1. *How we want to appear to others* (the image we hope to project).

2. *How we DO appear to others* (how well or poorly we come across)

3. *Who we really, deep down, truly are* (regardless of our desired image or the reception we receive).

Everyone has these three heads, and each of us juggle and reconcile our emotional priorities differently.

Image-conscious people, for example, make most of their decisions based on serving Head #1, which is preoccupied with how they appear to others. They react to Head #2 based on how they are treated by others. Stress comes from clashes between the image they want to project and the responses they receive.

A person's upbringing during his or her formative years (ages 0-to-13) greatly influences future adult behavioral tendencies. After the age of 13, significant emotional events—life's biggest positive experiences and most devastating negative traumas—trigger deep introspective reassessment. These life-changing emotional impact issues reshape behavioral choice as life unfolds.

For example, if you are old enough to remember back to 2001 and the *9/11* terrorist attacks on the World Trade Center and Pentagon, a seismic negative emotional event was unexpectedly forced among all Americans.

Reactions were dramatic and wide sweeping. American flags flew everywhere. Volunteerism went up, charity giving skyrocketed, divorces rose (as did births), and people quit jobs they didn't like to pursue something more fulfilling.

Everyone processed the same tragic emotional stimulus—a surprise attack on American soil—and reacted based his or her emotional priorities. People's reflexive actions were all across the board because everyone juggles his or her three heads differently.

To understand others (and us) more effectively, it helps to accurately read how they or we prioritize these three heads. Once we understand which head matters most—whether that is how we appear to others, react to others, or deep down who we truly are—we better understand what causes positive and negative feelings.

Why this matters at work

From a workforce perspective, early-career workers usually focus on how they want to be perceived. Mid-career workers vary the most, since their heads can be anywhere, with priorities often vacillating between all three heads. Veteran workers tend to accept where they are in life and career.

Maturity matters, too. Business maturity is a good indicator that someone has a strong sense of self. Conversely, immaturity is a tipoff that someone is so preoccupied with projecting and protecting his or her image that self-awareness Head #3, the one that owns who he or she really is, is either lost or on vacation.

Why 3-headed awareness matters more than ever

One reason life is a challenge is that all of us, whether we like it or not, must juggle. Experience may change which head matters most, but everyone juggles all three. Some do it well, others quite poorly.

For a young person growing through his or her formative years, puberty triggers a move away from the protective umbrella of a parent or guardian and image becomes *everything*. Head #1—how he or she wants to appear to others—influences decisions related to fashion, friendships, and social media. Image projection, plus the reactions of others who react to that desired image, becomes the focus of identity and self-worth. Because image projectors seek validation, rejection causes tremendous stress.

Cyber-bullying, for example, is emotionally devastating when a person or group of people dog-pile on top of an emotionally vulnerable person anxiously seeking acceptance. Teenagers are tremendously at risk to "haters" because teens have not yet learned how to face self-worth challenges by drawing strength and confidence from Head #3, who they truly are. They want to but cannot control what others think.

We see this pain throughout the emerging LGBT community, as well as among less confident teens and young adults trying to navigate an emotionally vulnerable time of life. There is no defense against a cyber-bully, which is why social media is increasingly being considered more of a negative influence than positive.

Selfies feed image projection and "Likes" are a statistical measurement of acceptance. People consumed with scorecarding these activities are more emotionally accessible and vulnerable to the uncontrollable opinions of others than those who do not care.

Because life can get stressful in a hurry when we are consumed by image projection and the pursuit of validation, things simplify when greater emphasis is invested in self-awareness. Along those lines, romance novelist Doris Mortman once said something I read in a quote book and never forgot.

"Until you're happy with who you are," she said, "you'll never be happy with what you have."

The journey from being preoccupied by Head #1 and Head #2 at the expense of where it needs to be, Head #3 (our true selves), can be difficult. For a parent, wanting to help a child along the path of self-discovery is a noble aspiration but it is up to the child to make the journey. Emotional maturity, self-confidence, problem solving, and coping skills are signposts that mark progress along the way.

When we look at how technology is changing behaviors, it is plainly evident that digital dependence and addiction do more harm than good. Balance and happiness radiate from the inside out, so when the head and heart are aligned, Head #3—who we really are—puts us exactly where we want to be.

But when head and heart are misaligned, we will be stressed and unhappy. *You can fool the head from time to time, and you can fool the heart from time to time, but it is really hard to fool both for very long.*

Digital meanness and cyber-bulling are sinister evils whose pain is determined by how mean the haters attempt to be and how emotionally vulnerable the recipient is. Another quote I keep in plain view in my writing room reads, "Even the strong are broken in places." If and when mean people figure out where to twist the knife, it hurts.

Cyber-bullies use meanness to emotionally wound and sometimes kill a young man or woman, whose tragic emotional vulnerability was that he or she had not yet learned how to juggle their three heads.

Teach those you care about the three-headed concept and the importance of learning to juggle. Behavioral awareness is key when minimizing the impact of bullies upon victims. Education and life skills, especially when tied to the cause-and-effect of pain caused by torpedoes to Maslow's Level #3 (Acceptance, Love, and Belonging) or Level #4 (Respect) help neutralize digital vulnerability.

3-headed Juggling Questions & Answers:

1. *"What challenges do we face when dealing with someone who is consumed by Head #1, How he or she wants to appear to others?"* When someone is consumed by image projection, he or she is totally divorced from who, deep down, he or she truly is. This is a risky place because all anyone can control are his or her choices and behaviors tied to projecting that image. He or she has zero control whether or not others see them as intended. We judge ourselves by our intentions. Others judge us by our actions, and gaps between the two create stress. For example, what is intended to project as confidence by a sender might be seen as arrogance by a receiver. Neither is right or wrong, the two simply see things differently.

2. *"What different circumstances arise with someone whose primary focus is Head #2, How he or she appears to others?"* The perception of others is uncontrollable, so worrying about it is pointless. People have good days and bad days and will think whatever they want. Becoming consumed by hoped-for acceptance is emotionally and physically dangerous. Coach the person out of here and toward Head #3, who he or she truly is. If someone is tremendously vulnerable to criticism, there is a good chance he or

she has a narcissistic personality disorder. Seek professional advice on how best to deal with it.

3. *"How are things different when interfacing with someone preoccupied with Head #3, Who they really are?"* When someone knows him or herself quite well, they will not be nearly as vulnerable to the meanness of others as if they were preoccupied by a constant craving for approval. This is a good place to be. A strong sense of self, with head and heart aligned, is the best platform for a confident, well-balanced persona.

Unhappiness on Campus

Statistics provided by the American College Health Association pertaining to suicide contemplation and follow-through are ominous. America has 18 million students on its college campuses, a number expected to increase to 20 million in the next eight years, and coping deficiencies are rising.

Too many think about it

In the past year, six percent of undergrads and four percent of graduate students in four-year schools have "seriously considered attempting suicide." Nearly half told no one.

To put this in context, in a very small class one student mulls ending his or her life. In auditorium-sized core lecture classes, which often range between 300 and 1,000 students per session, the tormented project to number between 18 and 60. When a bus would be needed to transport acutely troubled young adults, all of whom are theoretically there to experience four of the most fun years of their lives but instead contemplate ending it, clearly the problem cries out for solutions.

The problem is worsening

The suicide rate is increasing. Back in a more innocent era, the 1950s, only one-third as many students felt this way. Suicide is now the number two cause of campus fatalities, trailing only alcohol-related deaths. The 37 percent who reach out for help-most do not-is twice the number measured in 2000.

Emotional health is declining

The emotional health of college freshmen has declined to its lowest level since an annual survey started collecting data 25 years ago. Recent surveys of college counseling centers reveal that more than half their students have severe psychological problems, an alarming 13 percent increase in just two years. The

Center for Collegiate Mental Health at Penn State identifies anxiety and depression as the top two.

Stress triggers are many. Among the biggest:

1. Classes

2. Homework

3. Grades

4. Money, which includes tuition, loans, and family debt

5. Housing and social logistics

6. Competition. The harder a school is to get into, the more competitive its students tend to be.

7. Permeating doubt and lack of confidence concerning a perceived weak and unpromising job market.

Kevin Kuntz, a mental health counselor and expert in college campus issues, is concerned that too many students internalize their struggles. He estimates that nearly half of all college students are so depressed that at some point they have trouble functioning.

Pete Goldsmith, dean of students at Indiana University, shares Kuntz's concern. "It's a huge transition and all the support systems are different," he said. "For students who have lived in very structured situations and environments, going to a college campus-when very suddenly they have this new kind of freedom and new choices to make-it can be pretty overwhelming."

While it is worth noting that college suicides occur at half the rate of the general age group, many officials attribute the difference to the relative scarcity of guns on campus as compared to the street, where weapons are far more prevalent.

Each year approximately 1,100 students-roughly 7.5 per every 100,000-end their lives. One in twelve has at some point made a suicide plan, with 1.5 of every 100 making an attempt. Two young men die for every woman but women try more often. Men choose more violent means.

Contributing emotional factors also include family history, mental health challenges like depression and substance abuse, and easy access to harmful enablers. Interpersonal isolation, antisocial behaviors, performance difficulties, and sleeplessness are also clues.

Why support helps

Parents and friends should stay visible and supportive, especially during difficult times. It also helps to coach the despondent on the importance of sleep, diet, and exercise as enablers to a more positive place.

A student survey at the University of Akron drew 12,315 respondents and revealed that each year the vast majority of students, more than four out of five, will at times feel overwhelmed and exhausted. More than half feel lonely, nearly half feel immense anxiety, 60 percent become very sad, and nearly 40 percent feel great anger. Three in ten feel so depressed they find it difficult to function.

With this many negative emotions flooding the coping brain, it is not surprising to learn that five percent, one student in 20, have intentionally self-injured themselves.

While no one ever knows for sure the precise tipping point to tragic finality, a 2009 national survey of 302 counseling center directors pointed at these five reasons:

- 80 percent were depressed.

- 44 percent had relationship problems.

- 15 percent had academic problems.

- 27 percent were on psychiatric medication.

- 18 percent had previous psychiatric hospitalization.

Among the behavioral reasons Suicidology.org cited for these catalytic triggers are academic and social pressures, feelings of failure, alienation, and the lack of coping skills. Together they shaped emotional conclusions of stress, sadness, depression, and hopelessness-none of which leads to happy endings.

The Mask

In July 2015 New York Times reporter Julie Scelfo wrote a powerful piece about the widespread nature of campus unhappiness. In it she revealed that sometimes the university may be partly culpable, especially those that stoke a competitive culture. While acute competition creates academic stress, increasing numbers of students were feeling even more pressure outside the classroom, courtesy of social media.

The happy lives of others, wallpapered via smiling selfies, creates illusions of personal or social inadequacy. Nor does it help when the campus culture expects everyone to wear a "happy face" of false bravado, which further feeds the widespread reluctance to seek help.

High profile examples include the student bodies at Duke and Stanford. More than a decade ago Duke reported the stress its female students felt due to what it termed pressure to be "effortlessly perfect." The image to project, and boxes to tick, included smart, accomplished, fit, beautiful, and popular—all accomplished with seemingly no effort.

Stanford called it "Duck Syndrome." A duck appears to effortlessly glide across the pond, all the while paddling furiously beneath the surface to maintain propulsion.

Herein lies what many consider the heart of the problem, which is maintaining a positive front despite growing angst between the ears. Recalling what we discussed earlier about juggling three heads, this is a perfect example of how the preoccupation with Head #1 (how we want to appear to others) supersedes Head #3 (who we really are). We are hurting. We pretend we are not.

William Alexander, director of counseling and psychological services at the University of Pennsylvania, has noticed a pronounced shift in student coping abilities.

"A small setback used to mean disappointment," he said, "or having that feeling of needing to try harder next time. For some students, a mistake (now) has incredible meaning."

The reason may be two-fold, the first anchored in social psychology specialist Leon Festinger's 1954 social comparison theory. Festinger theorized we determine our worth based on how we stack up against others.

The second reason mistakes seem bigger is far more modern. Today mobile devices deliver a constant barrage of comparisons, collated from a wider pool of sources.

There is a big difference between not doing well and a diminished self-worth that says, "I'm no good." Failing at something differs from being a failure, but given the increasingly fragile emotional state of students on campus, it seems prudent to conclude this line is being blurred.

To solve what is happening on campus we must also examine the behaviors involved in getting there. In the view of New York Times columnist Frank Bruni, who watched years of what he termed "insanity" around the application process before writing about it, parents are partly to blame. Bruni cited overbearing helicopter parents for fostering cultural dynamics of perfectionism and overindulgence, which in turn have produced a huge pool of adolescents leaving the nest ill-equipped to fail en route to grand expectations of quick success.

Julie Lythcott-Haims, Stanford's dean of freshmen from 2002-2012, noticed this too.

"They could say what they'd accomplished," she said, "but they couldn't necessarily say who they were." She also noted the detrimental affect of over-parenting. Columnist Scelfo described this as lawnmower parenting, referring to those who "go beyond hovering to clear obstacles" such as enrolling in classes, contacting professors, and meeting with advisors. What bothered Lythcott-Haims most was not that parents were doing these things, it was that students were grateful and not embarrassed.

Lythcott-Haims first shared her observations in a 2005 op-ed piece for the Chicago Tribune. In it she cited three student shortfalls: a lack of self-awareness, the inability to make choices, and difficulty coping with setbacks. She termed this troika "existential impotence" and pointed to well-intended but misguided parenting. A subject matter expert, her book "How to Raise an Adult: Break Free of the Overparenting Trap and Prepare Your Kids for Success" is an excellent resource for those who wish to learn more.

Psychologist Alice Miller, whose seminal work in the late 1970s still resonates with therapists, described today's problem with a still relevant, decades-old explanation. She wrote, "In what is described as depression and experienced as emptiness, futility, fear of impoverishment, and loneliness, can usually be recognized as the tragic loss of self in childhood."

The *lost self* is the third head we juggle-who we really are.

The "net/net" of campus unhappiness

In view of rising enrollments, campus competition for admission, and expected high performance, plus the fact that elite colleges frown upon time off with few guarantees for readmission, we may not be able to change the rules of the game.

Help will come from better preparing sons and daughters to play the game differently. If a young man or woman enters this boundary-widening stage of life fully cognizant of who he or she is, and is not, and worries less about projecting images or how he or she is perceived by others, he or she will be better able to look at, analyze, and deal with setbacks while keeping each in its proper perspective.

Challenges abound in college and beyond, so rather than perceiving them as torpedoes to the engine room of happiness, students should be thinking, "Spitballs at a battleship." The book's final section, What to Do Today, provides the skills to get there.

Technology's Influence on World Politics

2016: The Summer of Political Discontent

History will describe the summer of 2016 as an explosive year of voter unrest. Straddling opposite shores of the Atlantic, pent-up frustration boiled inside American and British voters. Decorum at the heartbeat of the world's number one and number five economies ruptured arteries, and snake venom spurted everywhere. Confrontations between racial factions and law enforcement increased, as did ethnic mistrust. Hemorrhaging worst of all was traditional civility between candidates and emotionally divided electorates. Hope and optimism bled out, replaced by IV mixtures of anger and disrespect.

Earlier we reviewed the impact of technology on behavior and happiness and learned that the hottest flames stoked by changing behaviors negatively impacted Abraham Maslow's categories of acceptance and respect. So, when we step back and examine what specifically is powering the nuclear furnaces of political frustration throughout America and the United Kingdom, technology's influence is readily apparent.

The Internet has no rules, so traditional boundaries of voter engagement, accountability, accuracy, and party civility were supplanted by anonymous vitriol, self-serving untruths, and loud sound bites of character assassination. It was an ugly summer that provided little hope for positive discourse.

Barack Obama introduced global politics to the power of the Internet in 2008, but Obama entered the digital game at its virginal onset. He used the web to raise money and spread a message of hope and change, which resonated across virtually all voter demographics.

Eight years later the wired world is stunningly different. The web is ubiquitous. Once campaign strategists trolling for voter hot buttons discovered that uncontrolled immigration struck a nerve, they pounced like lions on a downed zebra. Nationalism via exclusion and self-determination superseded the more altruistic approach of advancing the collective good. This was the same key issue that British Boomers rallied around to shock the world and win the vote for BREXIT exodus.

In America a rude, derisive, and politically inexperienced self-promoting salesman blew up conventional Republican politics with bombastic proclamations that inflamed emotion. His unorthodox approach carpet-bombed the political establishment, yet seemed perfectly tailored for the spontaneous combustion of Internet communication, free advertising, and percolating blue-collar voter frustration.

His opponent, a career politician, has what every lifer in public service has: scars and skeletons. Attacks on her are relentless, easily spread by a medium that requires no fact checking or truth in reporting.

Voters, understandably, got confused. The two scored record low likeability ratings, and millions of undecided voters were left not knowing who or what to believe. This was a perplexing bewilderment as the election for the world's most powerful office rolled inexorably closer.

Millions of opinions easily bury the facts and neither American candidate is well liked or trusted but one will be elected. Once he or she is, there will be no unifying relief. Post-election America will remain just as angry and divided.

Across the pond, the post-BREXIT vote ushers in a new, unexpected reality: A new, no-nonsense Conservative Prime Minister, Theresa May, has to wade through generational schisms that smoke-bombed the United Kingdom and forced dramatic change.

The U. K. imports everything and exports very little, so cutting one-off trade deals without leverage or scale will not offset the almost immediate (and future) loss of jobs. The British Pound depressed against the U. S. dollar and faces a Herculean uphill climb.

Immigration was, and will remain, a huge voter influence factor in both political realms, which makes it worth revisiting Maslow's five-stage Hierarchy of Needs:

1. Survival

2. Comfort

3. Love & Acceptance

4. Respect

5. Self-actualization.

Internet access and social media pontification have stoked emotional fires on both sides of the immigration issue at every Maslow stage.

From an immigrant's perspective, Survival triggers a basic instinct. To a current resident, the abrupt and disorderly intrusion of uninvited foreigners is a strong emotional negative. Once immigrants-legal or otherwise-gain a foothold in a new country, their next logical pursuit is Maslow's second level: Comfort. This is a safe assumption. Who doesn't want a better life? We all do.

But Comfort requires immigrant footholds, which are often strongly perceived by longtime citizens as social subtractions, since an immigrant's advancement must logically decrement opportunity for others.

Maslow's third stage, Love & Acceptance, also creates conflict. If an immigrant works hard to assimilate but is denied acceptance because of a birth, cultural upbringing, or political stigma over which he or she has zero control, this lack of social acceptance creates close-minded cliques of like-minded people.

Instead of becoming neighbors who openly support each other and peacefully co-exist, the opposite happens. People judge more, understand less, pursue private agendas, and no one gains a thing.

Maslow's fourth level, Respect, is a curved lens through which the U.K. and U.S.A. see immigration differently. In the United Kingdom, older voters engineered the BREXIT secession from the European Union largely because immigration was, in their collective opinion, uncontrolled and disorderly. British tradition is nothing if not orderly, and when old Britain collided with open border Britain, change came too swiftly for the oldsters to manage.

Arriving immigrants did not care about British rules and decorum, and a majority of British voters did not care for the immigrants' lack of respect for British values and expectations.

In America, the disgruntled voting populace felt disrespected due to a blatant lack of teamwork by elected bipartisan officials. Sick and tired of narrow-minded party politics by lifer politicians who seemed to do nothing but collect a check, enjoy benefits, and hoard special interest perks, once candidates Bernie Sanders and Donald Trump tapped into voter frustration, both hit the mother lode. Voters came alive. Sanders preached compassion; Trump put immigration in the crosshairs of racist bombast. Voters had a hot-button issue worth digging in. Because immigration was a tipping point issue in the U. K., Trump was soon proclaiming it was a disaster in America too. He stabilized his white Boomer voter base, from which he could pivot without risk of voter defection, and followed the BREXIT blueprint to narrow a double-digit gap in the polls.

Trump's incendiary approach and Sanders' rabble-rousing enabled both to find an audience. Trump took full advantage of electronic media-which cost him nothing-to generate a mother lode of free publicity. An ad in the American gridiron football championship-the Super Bowl-cost $5 million for 30 seconds of airtime. A private businessman who claims riches he refuses to prove, Trump is a master brand builder who has parlayed his bombast into billions in free publicity.

Sanders, a refreshing alternative to a Clinton-weary nation, mobilized younger Democratic voters. Millions detested "politics as usual" and thumbed their noses at Trump for his mean, exclusionary, and separatist view of a nation that is no longer a melting pot but rather a stir fry of modern social diversity. Issues like global warming and sexual individualism also hit home.

Because of the Internet's flowing fountain of unpoliced spittle, anyone with a keyboard can raise a voice and this is where the 2016 Summer of Discontent deviates from previous campaigns.

In 2008 the Internet was a curious novelty. Today hundreds of millions have made an effort to be heard, especially through social media, which helped political parties in both countries backslide into a mucky swamp of cynical negativity.

Why this matters

"Voice of one" is significant because in the pre-Internet days information flowed primarily one-way. Messages were constructed by fact-based reporting and pushed out through credible news sources to the receiving public through conventional, controllable means that respected trust-based boundaries.

News items were collated, culled, crafted, and fact-checked prior to dissemination. There was an election *process*, and that process (for the most part) had rules both sides were expected to follow.

Those days are gone. There are no rules, nor governance, and everyone is free to say whatever he or she wants. Because the line between fact and fiction has been erased noise blurs, making it virtually impossible for crowded heads to sift through the garbage and find the recyclables. Opinions are shaped by whatever channel or channels someone happens to dial into which, as we mentioned earlier, are extraordinarily limited and heavily influenced by feeds customized based upon social analytics.

So, the net/net for both countries is that the future will be determined by those most adept at manipulating Maslow's fourth level: Respect.

The danger, of course, is that politicians who stoke anger through disrespect deem getting elected more important than governing based upon issues, facts, impact, and results.

BREXIT voters acted upon their feelings toward sovereignty by voting to leave the European Union. Most ignored the post-vote consequences, both short and long-term, specifically as their nation's strengths and weaknesses relate to an increasingly global economy. Major challenges loom for job retention and any semblance of robust economic sustainability.

A clear majority of dissatisfied American voters will go to the polls and vote for their president based on negative emotions. Voting booths will be emotional places, not logical ones, and that does not bode well for the result.

Regardless who wins, voters will remain dissatisfied. Vitriol will spew, haters will blame, and the odds that a president elected by an angry, divided populace can bring an agitated country together seem very long indeed.

We live in a world of new high stakes political reality that technology has changed forever. Tech's rising power and extraordinary global influence on voter behavior are, to say the least, somewhat disconcerting.

Chapter 3

Where We Are Headed

At the age of 17 I left home in Severna Park, Maryland and steered a rust-bucket van I'd bought for $350 roughly 750 miles south to Jacksonville, Florida. Off for college and antsy to go, I was gone for good, assuming we do not count the boomerang back after an ugly romantic breakup four years later, the fireworks from which are best saved for later.

I owned that van for just a few months but we shared several dramatic moments, the first of which came at the vehicle inspection station when I was trying to qualify for tags so I could legally roll the rattletrap in public.

This was my first trip to the inspection station and I misunderstood the inspection officer's instructions. He said, "Back up, go four-to-five miles an hour, and hit the brakes when I signal."

I got the 'Back up' okay but thought he said *"forty-five"* miles an hour and sent him diving for his life when I floored that old van and headed into the narrow inspection bay, jammed on the brakes—much to my surprise there were some—and slid the rear-end sideways to a dramatic halt reasonably close to the target line.

I did not pass the inspection. But I did get a "temp tag," which let me drive for ten days before I had to come back and fail again. I did this three times in a row.

That rattletrap somehow made it to Florida but when I arrived in Jacksonville I ran into traffic. Since the van's stick shift was on the column, starting and stopping kept me busy shifting up and down. Five miles shy of my destination I shifted from first gear into second. This proved a tactical error, as the shift arm broke off. I held it aloft in horror.

I was doomed to the stress of second gear purgatory in stop and go traffic for the rest of my drive, but for some reason kept holding the detached gearshift aloft, like a shocked actor who had just been handed an Oscar.

Those were challenging times, the salad days of youth. Problem solving skills were still in incubation, so each new challenge was a head scratcher.

Within a week I had secured a job in a grocery store near campus and worked my way through college as a meat cutter. It was a great job. I was a tradesman at 18, ate well, was paid well-enough to cover the cost of college and a modest, simple life-and was steadily employed for the next four years.

The meat department rescued me in the classroom. I faced a major dilemma in my freshman biology final, but knowing how a pig was put together saved me from academic probation. I was clueless where the 20 or so anatomical mysteries the teacher wanted me to identify were located-oddly named things like vena cava and pyloric valve-but I was quite certain how the pig was put together.

Rather than randomly harpooning numbered flags in the wrong places with hopeless guesses, I took my scalpel and laid out the little guy out just like you'd see him in the grocery store: teeny-weenie hams, teeny-weenie pork chops, miniature spare ribs-all of it. The teacher loved it and we cut a deal: He would give me a C if I promised to never take science again, a win/win solution that worked well for both of us.

Days drag but calendar months fly and four years after rolling onto campus holding aloft my dilapidated van's stick-shift, graduation loomed. The night before I sat down, studied my scarred hands, and tallied the numbers:

a. Four years, 24 stitches, two trips to the emergency room.

b. Side of left ring finger: gone.

c. Tip of left thumb: shortened but skillfully reshaped by plastic surgeon.

d. Pork chops cut: 250,000.

e. T-bone steaks: 13,000.

f. Personal best time cutting a whole frying chicken into all nine pieces-wings, thighs, legs, breasts, and back-26 seconds.

That job, becoming a meat cutter in a grocery store, taught me many important things beyond anatomy and cutlery. The biggies were time management, the power of hard work and hustle, dealing with people (nice ones and grumps), and what it was like to bust your stones and truly earn a living.

When the day came to hang up my white coat and bloodstained apron for the final time and collect my last check, I walked out knowing I would always be grateful for everything that labor-based job had done for me.

What's ahead: Robotics

Today the grocery store meat department is different. Teenagers are not afforded opportunities to learn a trade while working their way through school.

Local meat cutters no longer disassemble cows, pigs, lambs, and chickens. Meat on the hoof is processed regionally, pre-packaged and shipped out to stores. The business is now a hub-and-spoke distribution industry.

Immigrants, legal and otherwise, do much of this work. Fixed station, assembly line knife work is hard and dangerous, with all the fun stripped away. Meat processing is a monotonous, dangerous, output oriented, hurry and keep up occupation.

I was lucky to work in a comparatively golden era, complete with customer interaction, a wide variety of tasks to perform, and lots of fun times. By contrast, assembly line blade slashing is inglorious and boring.

This is blue-collar work performed by unskilled labor, but the money earned by the men and women who do it provides a life. Today the industry employs a half-million people, the vast majority being African-Americans, black immigrants, and Latinos. Most are women.

Soon these workers, who toil hour after hour inside arena-sized processing floors, may be out of work. The reason why is robotics.

Robots are ideal employees in blue-collar industries. They never sleep, are not paid overtime, and do not suffer horrific repetitive stress injuries. Deboning chickens will come first, as the animals are roughly the same size. Efficiency will increase, as even a one-percent increase in meat to market is worth hundreds of millions. Cows and pigs provide different challenges, as their bone structures vary, but the end-goal will be the same: more revenue at lower cost.

Robotic research in the meatpacking industry is focused on two things, algorithms and machine learning. It is safe to assume scientists will successfully solve for both.

The permanent loss of blue-collar jobs to robotics is not just a U. S. projection, but also one with global ramifications. Global unemployment will be affected as well, especially for younger, unskilled workers trying to enter the workforce. Jobs will be harder to come by, with good paying ones scarce.

Bill Gates, when asked to share his view on robots and robotics, wrote, "I think robots that have vision and manipulation as good as humans is a huge milestone that will happen in the next decade and is being underestimated."

Knowledge workers may escape, but the rubber band will continue to stretch between the life experiences of white-collar and blue-collar workers. Social frustration seems certain to rise.

Money never sleeps

While the meatpacking industry looks for ways to leverage technology to make more cash, industries that handle and move money are doing the same.

Cardless ATMs loom as a future trend that is now on our doorstep. Cardless opens up new ways to efficiently move money, whether from person to person, dealing with rewards, or processing promotional incentives.

Citibank is experimenting with biometrics that utilize eye scan technology. While this may be easier to master in a lab than marketplace-where logistics to capture millions of retinas may provide an initial challenge-the direction is clear. Mobile banking versatility will continue to expand and technology, via smart phones, will become even more ubiquitous than it is today.

The future of mobile technology

Now that the marketplace has accepted the speed of 4G technology, carriers and tech companies are hard at work on the next frontier, 5G. This is not a modest tweak, as this research is looking to bring speeds more than 100 times faster than current technology to the marketplace.

New York Times columnist Mark Scott recently wrote about 5G and shared the work being done south of London in the small town of Guilford. Here researchers at the University of Surrey are developing 5G that would enable students to download entire motion pictures to their phones in less than five seconds. Today, with 4G, the same download takes up to eight minutes.

The impact of 5G is wide-ranging. Driverless cars become much more practical, as do remote-controlled drones. Companies could also connect millions of devices like smart watches and home appliances.

The research is headed by Dr. Rahim Tafazolli, who says, "A lot of the technology already works in a laboratory environment. Now we have to prove it works in real life."

As Mark Scott points out in his article, the global hunger for ever-faster download and processing speeds seems insatiable. Powerhouse carriers such as AT&T and Japan's NTT DoCoMo want to be first to market. Infrastructure suppliers like Ericsson in Sweden and Huawei in China has fueled research worth billions into the field because they would gain from upgrading mobile Internet infrastructures. Google is also eyeing the technology, angling for a place to play.

Scott points out that although a global standard for 5G will not be settled until 2019 at the earliest, lobbying is already underway. This is a logistical puzzle with a mountain of pieces, so 5G probably will not arrive on the global scene until mid-next decade with consumer impact soon after. Both carriers and governments are eyeing 5G tests at global sporting event showcases like the 2018 Olympics and World Cup.

While much of the third world remains unwired, and densely populated areas such as South Korea operate at broadband-like speeds, the reason for the push is simple. Thomas Husson, an analyst at Forrester Research, nets it out.

"A lot of this," he said, "is about carriers and equipment makers looking for new ways to make money."

Domestically Verizon and AT&T are engaged in exploring the space, both watching Google as a potential new shooter. With an increasing number of companies willing to invest umpteen millions in Dr. Tafazolli's work at the University of Surrey, the goal is to create a real-world success story. Dr. Tafazolli's team has created the perfect setting.

"In the race to 5G," he said, "everyone wants to be first."

Impending changes go beyond just the 5G frontier. Issues like data privacy, security, customer experience, and competition keep driving technology, especially in mobile, forward. With Millennials having such a powerful influence in the marketplace, businesses are looking to optimize operations, automate processes, improve customer experiences, lock down security nightmares, and maximize revenue opportunities.

According to a Dongean report in 2013, Millennials already have a purchasing power of $2.45 trillion—a number that will continue to rise. Businesses will provide what Millennials want, and what they want is more horsepower. Person-to-person and business-to-person touches will continue to increase, primarily through text. Strategy is clearly shifting to a "mobile first" approach.

Where Facebook is headed

Facebook CEO Mark Zuckerberg, who knows a thing or two about global social connection and whose on-line fiefdom is already larger than Chinese President Xi Jinping's, is looking to take virtual reality (VR) way beyond gaming. After buying Oculus VR, a gaming company, for $2 billion in 2014, Zuckerberg is creating a new team focused solely on what he terms "social VR."

Zuckerberg shared his vision at the 2016 Mobile World Conference in Barcelona.

"Pretty soon we're going to live in a world where everyone has the power to share and experience whole scenes as if you're just there," he said. "Right there in person."

A Facebook release echoes the boss's message: "In the future," it said, "VR will enable even more types of connection, like the ability for friends who live in different parts of the world to spend time together and feel like they're really there with each other."

There is little reason to doubt Zuckerberg's ability to execute on his vision. Facebook and Instagram have the largest mobile audience in the world and control (via apps) more than one of every five minutes U. S. users spend on mobile. Facebook's global community already exchanges more than 45 billion messages daily, plus an additional four billion video views. Due to the remarkable quantity of content Facebook archives, Zuckerberg is also eyeing Google as a possible target for search.

"A lot of what we can get at are recommendations on products, and travel, and restaurants and things that your friends have shared with you they haven't shared publicly," he said. "Those are questions we can answer that no one else can answer, and that's probably what we continue to focus on doing first."

Add it all up and the future seems bright for Facebook to lengthen its tentacles to further embrace and expand the size, engagement, influence, and loyalty of its burgeoning global audience.

The future of the television industry

The view from the sofa will soon change too. Media and entertainment wants are changing and a comprehensive study by consulting giant EY Global shared insight on what they called "a world where consumers are in control."

Their six chief storylines included:

1. Storytelling will evolve to make better use of an ominplatform environment.

2. Ubiquitous screens will demand greater content mobility.

3. Social dynamics and synergistic experience will drive more event-based viewing.

4. Innovation in program discovery and television controls will drive new techniques to cut through the clutter.

5. Bingeing will drive more innovation in measurement and personalization.

6. New entrants demanding unique content will drive innovation beyond the traditional studio system.

EY also pointed out that one of the challenges content providers face will be trying to figure out how to entice payment for product. They also foresee the need for providers to link their supply chains, customer experiences, and analytics in order to achieve success.

Television programming, they concluded, will become a much more highly personalized experience. Those that do this well will win. The rest shall lose.

Television sets and 4K screens

Futuresource Consulting reported that sales of TV sets with 4K ultra HD screens surpassed 30 million in 2015, a growth leap of 147 percent despite overall TV sales dropping 2 percent. The message is clear: Those with money upgrade, while those on a budget hang on.

Futuresource predicts smart TV systems in 4K and HD will continue to increase in popularity as image quality and Internet connectively rise in importance.

These units are, by comparison, expensive. As such the decision to buy is value-based, not price-based, and the growth in the sector aligns with the findings in EY's future prediction report. Consumers of means will pay premium prices for technology upgrades with customizable utility.

Word choice analytics & behavioral prediction

Martin Seligman, a founding father of positive psychology, teamed up with Google co-founder Larry Page to work in a new area of on-line research: word analysis. The hypothesis they opted to chase centered around a computer's ability to use a word analysis algorithm to predict happiness and wellbeing across time and space based on how people communicate on social media.

Their first finding was startling. Geographic areas of high tweet negativity directly correlated to areas of high heart disease, which statistically bridged emotional and physical health. Correlations are now being drawn concerning personalities, mental illness, and other physical maladies.

According to co-researcher Johannes Eichstaedt, who wrote about the work in *Scientific Mind*, these results open the door to a wide variety of behavioral analytics that users will populate but others will parlay.

Medical insight will result, which is good, but people who operate in the shadows will grab hold too.

Eichstaedt pointed out that intelligence agents, political candidates, and business sharks with profit-driven angles will be just as interested in targeted audience emotions.

For the most part, once social media users beat the keys and send messages, they will remain oblivious to what is happening behind the cyberspace curtain. What people say and how they say it will be scrutinized, analyzed, collated, and used by others. Behaviorists will know more about the contributor's personality, and his or her mental and physical state, than the person's closest friends.

Because of the strong medical link between emotional state and physical wellbeing, algorithm writers and researchers will live here, collecting, stratifying, and analyzing data. Psychologists have an extraordinarily huge global window to look through and the world market for exploitation is wide open. A Pew Research Center study shared that 65 percent of American adults use social media regularly, a 10-fold increase in the past decade. Ninety percent of young adults use social media and users over 65 have tripled in five years. The median age of Twitter users is 32, which is six years younger than the nation's population median. Tidal waves of personal data just keep coming.

Researchers realize and are adjusting for "social desirability bias," which is the bravado mask a person uses to present a skewed version of his or her true self when interacting online. Close friends tone this down a bit, which is why sites like Facebook strive to separate friends from acquaintances.

While challenges exist-things like the dumbing down and evolution of various languages, street slang, emoticons, message brevity trends, and ethnic slants-psychologists are using "machine learning" to translate. The process is quite effective, as demonstrated by the accuracy of targeted advertisements that suddenly pop up and follow us, regardless if we jump a page or log off and back on again later. The algorithms accurately predict what we are likely to buy.

Why this matters

Three takeaways seem obvious:

1. Because people are getting almost impossible to reach on landlines via call center outreach, new methods will be devised to accumulate data.

2. Since a billion people use social media with blind and blissful unawareness despite interactions that often make them sad, users share huge amounts of insightful personal data via statuses, Likes, and

comments. Any good linguist and smart algorithm writer can virtually dissect the creator's thought processes.

3. Facebook's move to expand opinion ratings beyond simply "Like" is for its and its advertisers' benefit, not ours. The company is collecting expanded user data by categorizing responses in seven degrees of emotion:

   a. *Like* is a positive affirmation.

   b. *Love* is a strong positive emotion.

   c. *Haha.* Laughter is a supportive positive emotion.

   d. *Wow* expresses a high impact emotion.

   e. *Sad* shares a negative emotion, and

   f. *Angry* expresses a very strong negative emotion.

4. The more we share, the more they know. The more they know, the more they have to sell.

5. This swift, expansive movement to social media insight analytics will help our health and wellbeing but harm emotional freedom through what many will consider unfair and clandestine emotional manipulation.

Summary

Technology will expand its societal permeation and continue to evolve via choice, speed, and ease of use. Insight gleaned from customer behaviors will be used to sell more effectively than ever before to unsuspecting customers.

The more we engage digitally, the more technologists will learn about preferences, spending habits, and passion points. Coupled with a steady rise in digital addiction, storm clouds are gathering.

Technology will keep moving closer and it will be a challenge to keep its influence at a safe arm's length. Devices will continue to saturate the populous in number and use and behaviors will continue to change. Some will be for the better, others for the worse. Week to week wage earners will struggle and the gap will widen between the affluent and poor but everyone will be touched by data analytics. Saleable insight has value at every level of the marketplace.

Maslow's Hierarchy, which we covered earlier when sharing how recent behavioral changes directly impact happiness and contentment, will remain a prudent guide for behavioral decision-making. The more you share, the more you'll be impacted.

The community of tomorrow: Empowering cities for sustainable wellbeing

A small group of forward-thinking society-shapers are using design methods that incorporate psychology, neuroscience, and big data to proactively offset the detrimental aspects of the Facebook Effect. The work is part of an emerging science on community motivation that strives to convert insight into positive behavioral influence.

Latvian computer scientist Dr. Agnis Stibe, a social engineer in the Persuasive Cities program at MIT Media Lab in Cambridge, is a driving force behind this innovative research. Dr. Stibe is acutely aware of the need to maximize positive interactions in order to offset the detrimental influence behavioral change can have on Maslow's two key levels, Level 3 (*Acceptance, Love, and Belonging*) and Level 4 (*Respect*).

Staying ahead of a tsunami the size of technology presents its challenges and opportunities, but Dr. Stibe's work specializes in designing communities of the future that include recommendations on how best to integrate technology's positive capabilities to shape desired behaviors.

A big part of future urban design turns a negative into a positive by converting roads in congested traffic areas into bicycling superhighways. In this regard, Europe is ahead of America. The first year London created its cyclist superhighway, bicycle ridership increased 70 percent.

Norway is advancing the concept much more dramatically, earmarking $1 billion—a huge investment for a small nation and the world's 15th largest oil producer—for its cycling infrastructure. Norway's plan is to build bike superhighways around its 10 largest cities, enabling navigation to and through the cities with direct routes to the suburbs. The capitol city of Oslo has already banned center city car traffic.

Dr. Stibe's goal is to help design cities that feel, understand, and care about people's wellbeing. Design factors include human activity, environmental conditions, and market dynamics.

According to Dr. Stibe, "Persuasive urban systems will play an important role in making cities more livable and resource-efficient by addressing current environmental problems and enabling healthier routines."

The end game is globally relevant urban lifestyle enhancement. Dr. Stibe explained the team is working on macro strategies for global impact.

"Drawing on socio-psychological theories and integrating them with new concepts for urban design, the persuasive cities research focuses on improving wellbeing across societies."

Rather than what he calls the old "carrots and sticks" behavioral influence tactics, the future design initiatives rely on social influence from crowd behavior. Done properly, says Dr. Stibe, "Continuous interplay can ultimately result in an ongoing process that reshapes communities and societies without any other incentives."

The intriguing design factor here is social influence, altruistically steered for people's betterment.

"Sensible cities employ sensor networks to read crowd behaviors," explained Dr. Stibe. "In other words, these cities feel human movements. These crowd behaviors further serve as an input for big data analytics that smart cities apply to classify groups of people according to similar behavior patterns or profiles."

When the desired best practices are identified, they can then be shared with other groups via intentionally designed socially influencing systems.

Dr. Stibe divides the populace persuasive cities will deal with into three categories:

1. *Self-contained.* These people are happy with who they are and what they do and are primarily change-averse.

2. *Self-driven.* These people have comparatively high levels of motivation and chase goals. Due to their self-starting nature, persuasion might not be required to create proactive movement.

3. *The January 1ˢᵗers.* These are people who would like to change their routines but have very little success doing so and is the segment most likely to benefit from the positive, supportive, persuasive approach.

With the population identified, the social influence system design involves solving challenges in three separate stages: engagement, participation, and involvement.

"Cooperation and social facilitation seem to be more effective to make individuals participate and do the envisioned future behavior, even without a formed attitude toward it," Dr. Stibe said. "Competition and recognition seem to be more effective in engaging the target group to do the future behavior as the principles focus on both attitude and behavior simultaneously."

What is especially encouraging with this approach is Europe's success with urban mobility, especially bicycling, for which Dr. Stibe is a big advocate.

"Cycling is good for the head and heart," he said. "Better for both than sitting in traffic."

Why this matters

Much of the book to this point has shared the history, direction, and roller-coastering behavioral positives and negatives associated with technology's evolution, advanced societal integration, and expanding permeation.

Smart people do clever things, and the work being done at MIT's grad school think tank is timely and relevant. Dr. Stibe's work, in collaboration with global thought leaders like Samir Chatterjee, Katja Schechtner, Matthias Wunsch, Alexandra Millonig, Stefan Seer, Ryan C.C. Chin, and Kent Larson, is making rapid advancements in the scientific pursuit of positive social change that embraces technology as the backbone of future society.

When visionary thinkers take what technology gives us, and leverage those things in positive ways for the designed betterment of society, we should draw confidence from knowing that they are on the case.

Positive change should result.

Chapter 4

What to Do Today

Technology is like an expanding set of in-laws. We can't control who they are or what they do, but we must deal with them regardless. Life requires digital coexistence, so the best way to manage habits and contentment may come from following these five guidelines.

1. *Know who you are.*

2. *Insist on and protect non-digital private time.*

3. *Stay acutely aware of your daily time choices.*

4. *Manage your Worry Circle.*

5. *Be resilient.*

1. Know who you are.

People are, by nature, herd animals. Among a flock of sheep, five determine their direction. If the leaders decide to go over a hill, the rest follow.

Technologists coax followers, so when it comes to digital engagement we can follow blindly or live a more self-aware life by making astute time choices to maintain our preferred behavioral and emotional balance. When we are acutely aware of how our behaviors are influencing our emotions, we are better able to protect the core of who we are and how we want to feel.

Happiness will not come from a projected image or specific number of Likes on social media. Happiness and contentment come from being comfortable with the third head we juggle, "Who we really are."

Because it is easy to lose our true selves in addictive habits, it helps to maintain a strong sense of self. When head and heart are aligned, and the mind is clear to make decisions that let us live with a positive rhythm, navigating time choices is simplified.

If visiting the real you is a place you haven't been for a while, it may help to invest some think time in who you want your third head to be. A simple exercise can help define who that person is.

The Daily Dozen is a prioritized list of 12 things that accurately describe your best self. This describes who you want to be, not who someone else says. This is an introspective exercise, so how deep you are willing to go determines how much time it requires. I wrote mine 25 years ago while sitting on a Bahamian seawall and it took four hours. This is an investment in you, not a trivial or hurried task, so when you invest the time to sort things out the list will hold true for years.

Behaviorally speaking, block out the first two heads of the 3-headed person—how you want to appear to others and how you do appear to others—and focus solely on the third, who you really are. In a perfect world, where you are living in a manner that makes you happy or content, what are the top 12 character traits that help define who you aspire to be?

All 12 of those traits are tucked away in your head and heart. Find them, list them, and polish their descriptions until each is defined perfectly.

Once you have your list, stack-rank all 12 in order of importance. Test each for truth, clarity, and priority. When you have perfectly described and sequenced all, you will know it. Print and post your list in plain view. I have one copy on my refrigerator and another in my writing room.

Your Daily Dozen is your road map. Over time, when you feel down or things are going a bit sideways, the list is there to help. Emotional disjoints often arise due to conflicts with one of your defined priorities. Identify what's busted and fix it.

A well-written Daily Dozen can guide you for years and adhering to what matters most helps you stay positive. Without a written definition of who you really are, your third head, a crowded cranium can seem like an ambulance trying to parallel park.

Technology can interfere because chronic use or misuse alters behaviors. We trade away some things that make us happy and efficient for things that cause stress or fatigue.

Guard against that. Protect the real you at all times.

2. Insist on, and protect, your daily (non-digital) private time.

Digital addiction is growing, as is addiction denial and "telepressure," the emotional feeling that we must be on call every hour of every day. Block time each day that is "your time." Your time is uninterrupted think time. No phone, no Internet, no tablet, no nothing. Read, write, meditate, work out, or walk the dog. Get back to you.

Separation anxiety is an interesting phenomenon in that young children have it when separated from their parents and parents get it when grown children leave the nest. Technology addicts have it when separated from their gadgets and smartphones.

Phones don't care; they will be wherever their owner left them whenever the owner returns. The world will not end if you are apart. Truth be told, the world will get along quite nicely because seven billion others on the planet could not care less.

Quiet time is think time and introspective think time is always good. Carve out a specific part of each day to get away from your gadgets and get back in touch with what you are thinking, feeling, and doing. If you have to, start small: one hour a day this week, two hours a day next week, or half-days on the weekend. Wean yourself to freedom.

If you sense that someone you care about struggles with digital separation, become familiar with the work of Dr. Dave Greenfield. The head of The Center for Internet and Technology Addiction, Dr. Greenfield has seven different addiction tests available on the organization's site (www.virtual-addiction.com). All are free, and among them is a test to determine whether or not children are too connected.

3. Stay acutely aware of your daily time choices.

Earlier we discussed the four ways waking hours pass by: We waste time, spend it on low-return activities, invest in things that matter, or cherish life's special moments.

With online time trends increasing in minutes per day, and future technologies designed to entice us to stay engaged even longer, periodically reassess what you are doing. Evaluate how much time you are spending being busy but not fulfilled or productive.

Results change only if time choices change. All of the super performers I have known and interviewed squeeze as much as they can out of every day and zealously protect their time. Because they live with self-managed urgency, their personal brands waste as little time as possible, which frees up more time for things with greater priority and payoff.

In many ways the Internet and apps are seductive time-wasters. Don't fall into the trap. Over time, smarter choices create positive accomplishments. Protect your time. Be aware of how it passes and make purposeful choices that inject the mind with positive emotions.

4. Manage your Worry Circle®.

Chronic digital engagement turns the mind into, for lack of a better term, "an open bar." Open bars are often chaotic affairs. A host throws a party so others can show up to eat and drink for free and guests take full advantage. People get loud, sloppy, and make a mess. But freeloaders don't pay for the mess, nor do they clean it up. The host is the one dealing with the damage.

Just because someone has access to your mind does not mean he or she has the right to be there. With more entry avenues into the brain than ever before, if you let noise and negativity in whenever it wants, both will stroll in and take a seat.

Crowded heads need not stay that way. Rather than letting your mind remain an open bar, treat your head like a castle protected by a surrounding moat and drawbridge. The drawbridge is raised and lowered as you decide. Worries are by invitation only.

When it comes to improving you life by worrying less about the wrong things, the best way to help yourself is by managing your Worry Circle.

The Worry Circle is the imaginary bubble inside your head that houses everything you worry about. Here is what you need to know:

- *It is normal to worry.* Everyone worries, so the trick to staying upbeat and positive is learning to manage the noise. The more effectively you learn how to manage what you should and should not worry about, the lower your stress level will be.

- *The need to worry is relentless.* Because the Worry Circle must stay full at all times, when one concern is resolved another takes its place. In this regard worries are portable; they come and go. Staying balanced relies on realizing that worries are transient and committing to yourself that you will protect your head by proactively managing what you choose to worry about.

- *What we worry about is largely a matter of choice.* As mentioned earlier, just because someone or something has access to your head does not mean that he, she, or it has the right to be there. We can embrace or reject every worry that tries to enter our minds. We are fully empowered to choose what stays inside our Worry Circles and what is not allowed.

People worry about three types of things and eight subcategories.

The three types of things are:

1. *Things your decisions and personal actions can control.*

2. *Things you can influence to some extent but not completely control.*

3. *Things you cannot control.*

Elaborations on these three are shared in a following table, *"How the 3 Types of Worries Affect the Mind."*

The subcategories

The eight subcategories of worries radiate outward from self, like splash rings from a pebble tossed into a pond. Multiple examples are shared in a second following table, *"Worry Circle Categories of Concern."* The eight include:

a. Self (health, well-being, happiness, consumption habits, etc.)

b. Relationships

c. Familial (marital, parental, sibling, children, relatives, etc.)

d. Friends

e. Work (boss, coworkers, workload, etc.)

f. Money

g. Social/Community

h. Societal.

5. Worriers beget worriers.

A son or daughter of a chronic worrier must learn to manage his or her head differently than how they were raised. Worry Circle management is a life skill, so anyone who decides to become really good at managing what he or she worries about can quickly learn to do so, regardless of their upbringing.

Once you have learned to better manage your worries, "Pay it forward."

Teach these techniques to others. School teaches a lot of things, but smart head management is not one of them.

The portability of Worry Circle priorities

Before the recession, America's number one Worry Circle issue was making money. When the economy collapsed, the nation's biggest worry switched almost immediately to having a job. Now, during the recovery, the workforce has stabilized and the big worry has changed again, this time to rebuilding wealth.

These pronounced changes in what we worried about during the 18-month pendulum swing between recession and recovery illustrate the portable nature of Worry Circle issues. Large or small, they come and go.

How the 3 Types of Worries Affect the Mind

Worry Type	Definition	Impact on the Mind	How to Handle
Controllable Our actions *can* address and remedy the concern.	Our thoughts and actions are capable of resolving the issue. *Example:* Going on a diet and losing weight.	*These are positive.* Controllable issue we want to embrace because controllable Worry Circle issues inspire action. When something bugs us enough to take action, and we can resolve it through our own behaviors, the process is positive and inspiring. Helps create life balance & boost confidence.	Own these. When something bugs you enough, take action. Resolve the issue. Being in control of everything that parks in your emotional air space is a great place to be. These are the worries you want to own. These are the ones that belong in the Worry Circle.
Influence We cannot solve the entire issue, but are able to control some portion or aspect of it.	Addressable but not solvable. Influence issues are part controllable and part uncontrollable. They are blends of both. *Example:* Parenting. We can set a good example, but children will do whatever they choose or their friends talk them into.	*Stressful and burdensome.* Fretting over things we cannot control in their entirety causes relentless worry. It is never good to carry around worries concerning things that cannot be controlled.	Because influence issues blend controllables with uncontrollables, own the part you can control and jettison the rest. Block the uncontrollable elements from your mind. All of us deal with influence issues. The smartest way to handle them is to separate them into what you can control and own it; and identify what you cannot control and block it from your Worry Circle.

Cannot control The problem is bigger than our ability to solve it.	Bigger than our ability to influence them, much less solve them. *Example:* The economy.	TOXIC! The mind mushrooms these things to their worst possible hypothetical extreme that almost never happens. These create very dangerous negative spirals, because none of the stress creators can be eradicated. Because these negative "what ifs" are irresolvable, the negative energy it takes to carry them around can be debilitating.	Refuse to ponder these. Deny entry or kick them out of your head. Uncontrollables should never be allowed to linger because you cannot solve them and they will haunt you. These create frustration, sadness, depression, and worse. Never let these types of worries fester. *Kick these out of your Worry Circle.* These are dangerous. Bar them from your mind's castle.

Worry Circle "Categories of Concern"

Common Examples of All Eight Categories of Worry

1. SELF	2. RELATION-SHIP	3. FAMILIAL	4. FRIENDS
health	happiness	health	health
stress	resilience	well-being	happiness
happiness	trust/mistrust	relationship(s)	well-being
sadness	friction	communication	touches
mortality	hard/easy	happiness	addictions
contentment	strengthen-ing/eroding	good influences	
fulfillment	doubt	bad influences	
decisions	commitment	role modeling	
ambition	communication	friction	
money	money	addictions	
weight	health	obligations	
appearance	appearance		
self-image	addictions		
self-esteem	values		
habits (good & bad)			

5. WORK	6. MONEY	7. SOCIAL/ COMMUNITY	8. SOCIETAL
job stability	generating	schools	causes
upward mobility	saving	neighborhood	ethnicity
financial rewards	investments	generational	religion
the boss	retirement	ethnicity	politics
coworkers	planned expenses	involvement	global warming
commuting	unplanned expenses	keeping up with the Joneses	other environmental
values	insurance	religious	,
ethics	cost of living		
personal growth	expense management		
professional growth	discretionary spending		
feeling valued	depreciating assets (ex. cars, boats, etc.)		
doing proud & valued work	Taxes, IRS, and audits		
frustrations	value of money		
perceptions	moochers		
	materialistic pursuits		

Worry Circle summary

It is hard to be happy if you are walking around with an overflowing Worry Circle. Statistically speaking, those who cannot effectively manage their Worry Circles are carrying around way too much of the wrong noise, 40-to-60 percent on average. Since half of what is in their Circles does not even belong, freeing themselves of unnecessary negative thoughts provides a quick and tremendously reassuring emotional boost.

Since we all worry, the trick to regaining or maintaining better balance is improving how we deal with the negative thoughts that troll our mind's entryway. If we allow in only what belongs, controllable worries, we will stay strong. If we overload with uncontrollable stress creators beyond our ability to remedy, their negative impact will wear us down.

We all have friends who seem upbeat all the time, while others carry the weight of the world. The difference is usually how they handle the Worry Circle. Upbeat people control their air space. This is a life skill worth mastering and incorporating into your personal brand. With awareness, discipline, and a commitment to a better self, Worry Circle management is instantly doable.

5. Be resilient.

By definition "resilience" involves flexibility and elasticity. The reason resilience is necessary is fear, which fuels negative thought and pessimism.

Change is more difficult for creatures of habit than those who look at new conditions as problems rather than opportunities. Some animals migrate—godwits, for example, are small birds that summer in New Zealand's southern hemisphere and then fly thousands of miles non-stop to summer again up in the Arctic Circle. Coyotes don't migrate, they adapt to urban sprawl. Polar bears have no such adaptable flexibility and are threatened because of it.

Technology will continue to change the world, so we must adapt to new devices and methods.

When we face perceived threats, our primal instincts kick in. These include flight, fight, and freezing. Unhappy college freshmen take flight. They transfer. Elephants, individually and collectively, confront attackers. Rabbits freeze, hoping to conceal themselves.

Way back in 1898 Charles Darwin wrote that since fear is an emotion, three things happen in sequence. First the threatened creature focuses on what is relevant to the situation. Then the body prepares for action, which will take the form of flight, fight, or freeze. Lastly the animal archives memories, which enable them to accumulate and react in the future based upon past experience.

Processing what is salient to the situation depends on what our five senses tell us. From these sensory data collectors we draw conclusions. This is a challenge for college students, especially freshmen, because so many situations are new. The bigger the change, the more variables there are to process.

Fear in humans often connects two or more things almost automatically, which is not always good. Bad grades, for example, might trigger a direct association to the wrath of angry parents. Flashing police lights in the rearview mirror tie to a ticket, fine, points on the license, and higher insurance.

When deciding what to do the brain takes either a circuitous route or a very direct one. The circuitous route involves conscious evaluation and contemplation, from which a conclusion is derived.

The shortcut is, by nature, virtually reflexive.

Stressed out students are more likely to react reflexively. In a heightened emotional state, this can be a very dangerous way to worry about new predicaments. Children who have been reared without learning adequate problem-solving approaches will lack the ability to disassociate reflexive links. Those raised to think and evaluate options are better equipped to improve how they approach emotional problem solving.

Chronic stress is horrible for a number of physical reasons that contribute to a negative spiral. Stressors from the past blend with those of the present, projecting forward to expectations of negative future consequences.

In his popular book "Why Zebras Don't Get Ulcers," Stanford professor Robert Sapolsky explains why a zebra's approach to life should teach us how to better handle threats. Zebras worry only about immediate danger. They do not worry about the past or future. Zebras deal with what is in front of them at the time, often lions, and then return to grazing in the savannahs.

Without adequate coping skills, people cannot do this. Once caught in a downward spiral, the brain's ability to regulate emotions is harmed. Unhealthy or risky choices often result. This, of course, is happening on college campuses all over the world.

University of Denver resilience expert Dr. Kateri McRae works with the Institute for Brain Potential and offers hope.

"When it can be done in a safe environment," she said, "exposing yourself to a previously feared situation will encourage your brain to use its brakes and diminish bodily responding."

Safe, of course, is the operative word. Students who have unconditional support systems at home and on campus are better equipped to make good decisions than those who feel alone.

It is easy to say confronting fears is better than avoiding them, but all of us have confronted fears before. As kids we may have jumped off a high dive, done a somersault on a trampoline, or navigated heavy traffic while learning to drive a stick-shift car.

Because people often feel stress because they are not getting the results they hope for, it is important to remember the three reasons why performance problems exist.

- Someone *can't* do it. Because they are willing but not capable, this usually boils down to being a knowledge or skill issue. Knowledge can be taught and skills developed, so this one is often fixable.

- He or she *won't* do it, which stems from the lack of a perceived reward, the absence of a sufficient punishment, or the feeling that because they are really good at what's being asked they will get stuck doing more of it. This is frustrating to parent, coach, or manage through because *won't do its* are not skill issues, but simply a lack of "want to."

- Or the person is *prevented from* doing what is required. In these cases something gets in the way that prevents success. In learning, dyslexia is a great example. The student is willing, but has a barrier that must be worked around. I had degenerative hearing loss as a young man and virtual deafness that nearly ended my career at 26. My sister was born blind. Today she has dual masters degrees, lives in Florida, and runs a family counseling practice. What we had in common were two things, bad luck and very strong support systems. Support systems help people in need navigate workarounds. When highly visible and actively engaged, a non-judgmental support system will help a student remain focused on pursuing positive outcomes.

Stress inhibits creative thinking, so it always helps to challenge the source. Since we tend to find in life what we look for, when we look for the good in someone (or the life we are living) we see the good. If we look for the bad—whether in a job, relationship, situation, or life—we will see the bad. Negative emotional conclusions are drawn from accumulated evidence. Evidence is collected based upon what we are looking for.

Use contrarian thinking

Perspective often changes if we use what the Central Intelligence Agency (CIA) calls "contrarian thinking."

Contrarian thinking flips an assumption around. Whatever is assumed to be true is false and vice-versa. Agents are trained to assume both points of view are correct, and dissect each accordingly.

For example, instead of life being bad, assume life is good and list the reasons why. When someone spirals down into a negative place, one of the first things flushed is gratitude.

Gratitude is a positive enabler. Coach those you care about to write a list of things they are grateful for. The length of the list is not as important as the emotional refocus the exercise creates, which is building a conscious bridge from a negative place to one of positive awareness.

Without this type of guidance it is difficult for someone to snap out of a funk on his or her own. One gratitude reminder a day is fine.

Suppression

In her lectures on resilience, one of the key areas Dr. McRae focuses on is behavioral suppression, which today is an enormous problem on college campuses. Suppression can be culturally influenced, meaning that some societies raise their children to keep their feelings internalized. Verbal and non-verbal reactions are hidden, not expressed.

In times of high stress, suppression is harmful because we cannot help those who do not seek it or don't exhibit signs that sadness is building. Avoidance, distraction, and rumination also serve as inhibitors to emotion regulation.

"Those may backfire," said Dr. McRae. "Do more of things like reappraising and reframing the situation, actively problem solve, take action, and seek social support. Accept that challenges come and go."

Because the anxious mind stays in turmoil, expediency helps. We should not stand in quicksand, bemoaning where we are. We should pull ourselves out or call for help. Dr. McRae is an advocate for changing, not dwelling upon, the status quo. "Act quickly," she says. "It is the best way to avoid emotional uproar."

Reframing helps

When we change what we are looking for, we see different things. For example, many beachcombers enjoy strolling along looking for beautiful seashells. They find them. I never look for shells, I look for fossilized shark's teeth and find them. Photographers snap shots of seagulls, pelicans, sunrises, sunsets, and breaking waves. We walk the same beach but find different things because we *look* for different things.

Campus despair

Campus unhappiness generally stems from three things, sadness, anger, or guilt. Sadness is the biggie.

"Sadness," said Dr. McRae, "stems from an appraisal of loss. Usually people, relationships, expectations, visions of the future, and versions of self."

While all of these can crowd an impressionable Worry Circle, relationships come and go, expectations change over time, the future is uncontrollable, and strength of self comes from juggling our three heads effectively while making sure we protect the most important one of all, who we really are.

When head and heart are aligned, we are in a place to build. When those two are misaligned, climbing out of sadness is very hard to do.

How dopamine helps resilience

Dopamine is the body's "happy drug." When released properly, such as through laughter, intimacy, exercise, exhilaration, and feelings of achievement, dopamine helps fuel resilience. All of these help propel an upward spiral to a better emotional place. But if channeled from negative sources such as drug abuse, addictive texting, or aggression-based video games, these dopamine sources will perpetuate or worsen the downward spiral.

Positive change has its best chance of occurring when a "reward system" reinforces the desired behavior. Since bad habits must be overcome and good ones reinforced, positive associations with good rewards are important. The brain will stamp and embrace these rewards. Absent this type of positive emotional connection, chances are behaviors will not change.

Since dwelling in a negative place is often habit-driven, part of breaking an undesirable habit might involve a reframed approach to pleasure. For example, when we go to the movies, we often purchase a box of popcorn and shovel it in like it's a race to the bottom of the bag. When we go to a fancy restaurant and order a decadent dessert, we don't scarf it down, we savor each bite, nibbling as we go. We are much more acutely aware of the act, flavors, and experience of fine dining.

This cognitive awareness of being "in the moment" is important to resilience. Dwelling upon what is bad about the moment doesn't help, but having heightened awareness of what's *good* about the moment will. This is why an emphasis on gratitude for what we have, free of worry about what we do not, can have such a positive effect on resilience.

"Can't because" versus "How can we?"

Since thoughts drive emotional conclusions, a positive approach to daily challenges is far healthier than "Can't because." Optimists not only carry less baggage, the Mayo Clinic reports that optimists live 19 percent longer than pessimists.

How these two extremes, optimism and pessimism, perceive challenges is a good example of contrasting approaches to life. To an optimist, a setback is a temporary derailment and the will to continue is undeterred. To a pessimist, a setback is validation and the will to continue is diminished.

A person looking at life through a "can't because" lens would benefit from contrarian thinking. Flipping to a "how can I" approach will enable him or her to change focus from the current negative state to a more optimistic future. Yes, now might be a tough time. But if we focus on the fix with a *how can I* approach, this frustration will soon improve.

The elements of wellbeing

The World Health Organization identifies four ingredients to wellbeing:

a. A sense of aliveness and vitality.

b. Relationships and career satisfaction in harmony with one's personality style, aptitude, and skills.

c. A sense of belonging.

d. Feeling connected to something bigger than you.

Each of these ties to Maslow's Hierarchy of Needs, which we earlier mapped against the negative influence technology exerts upon multiple decreasing behaviors.

College, by nature of the beast, infuses drama into all four of the WHO's criteria. If one, two, three, or all four are damaged or missing from a young person's life, it is not surprising he or she feels sad and emotionally exhausted. Telling someone to "Snap out of it" or "Don't worry about that" doesn't help, nor does languishing in self-pity or being yelled at by a parent. Ignoring the emotional devastation that comes from a major breakup won't help, either.

Each of these four ingredients to personal wellbeing presents an action-based problem-solving opportunity.

This is a very smart generation, but coping and resilience are taught by the real world. Students must have or learn real-life coping skills in order to demonstrate resilience. Young adults will struggle if left to learn life skills on-line.

Teach a young person how to think and he or she will figure things out. Tell them what to do, but never explain why, and they very well may not.

Happiness vs. Contentment

According to a survey by Time Magazine, only 17 percent of people are happy all the time. Roughly 58 percent are "frequently happy," but 25 percent do not experience much happiness at all.

Moving from the unhappiness end of the spectrum to pure bliss may be an unrealistic expectation, so the answer may lie in the middle, which is contentment.

Dr. McRae calls this "life satisfaction," and says the real question is not if someone is happy as much as it is, "Are they content?" Contentment with life involves meaningfulness, but not necessarily overt happiness. Some by nature will never have a sense of humor, which is fine. Many have too many scars to laugh and that is okay too.

But if discontent is causing frustration or unhappiness, discontent is fixable. Each of us has a true north in life, and sometimes that means forking off onto a road that suits us but not others. Some of those treks may require hacking through the underbrush because no trail exists.

Courage and gumption help a person follow true north, but here again a positive support system certainly helps. Another propellant on the road to contentment should include a person's "go to" dopamine reward, as each of us needs a valued reward system to encourage us along the way.

Dopamine rewards motivate us to take action and broaden our cognitive repertoire. How broad those possibilities grow hinges largely on our emotional state. When we are in pursuit of something that truly matters, our range of positive thoughts increases. When we are in a negative place, perceived possibilities contract or disappear.

Contentment is a feeling, which means it comes from a positive emotional conclusion we have reached after processing multiple data points. To a person wallowing in discontent, contentment is a big picture destination that looms on a distant horizon with no easy shortcut. Getting there requires steps, and steps require a willingness to begin.

Laughter helps

Laughter is one of nature's best mood elevation tricks, so the ability and willingness to laugh at self or a situation is always beneficial. Here again an optimist may find laughter easier than a pessimist.

I mess up a lot, but when I do I try own and keep things in their proper perspective. "Well, I bungled that one," I will remind myself, "but on the plus side, a billion Chinese simply don't care."

What this go-to punchline does for me is help keep things in perspective. Laughter is a positive "stealth health" gambit that disrupts negative thinking. A person cannot stew in negativity if he or she is laughing.

One cup of sand at a time

When I bought my first house I inherited a huge pile of sand in the front garden. I felt like an ancient Egyptian facing the worksite to build a great pyramid. I never learned why the mini-mountain was there but once I closed on the house I owned it. The whole big pile.

Since I had no plan, the sand pile sat. Each night I hoped sand thieves would steal it but the rascals never came.

Every time I saw the thing, it bugged me. It bugged me in the morning when I left for work and bugged me again when I returned. It bugged me every time I looked out the front window. I never saw my lawn or shrubs, only the mountain of sand.

Days turned into weeks. One night I was talking to my father on the telephone, whining about the dune and he offered a suggestion.

"Every morning when you leave, take a cupful of sand from the pile and scatter it on the lawn."

The message was clear: Problems do not solve themselves without action. Instead of lamenting my sand hill, I reminded myself how lucky I was to own a home. I had a roof, heat, and food in the refrigerator. Sand was the least of my worries. The cup-a-day solution spurred me into getting rid of the thing. Looking back I wonder why the heck I waited so long to take action.

Students struggling with stress and sadness on campus are just like those of us dealing with it at home and work. Each of is dealing with our own big pile of sand. A good plan and positive support system that coaches helpful options will help move the mountain, even if it's just one cup a day.

Rumination doesn't help

Rumination, which involves dwelling on a negative emotion, won't move the sand. Nor will having a co-ruminator, a person who reinforces the negativity of the situation. Co-ruminators perpetuate (or worsen) the status quo.

People suffer. We all do. To feel that something is wrong with us when we feel down is a false assumption. Suffering is not a pathological weakness; it is the downside of life's rollercoaster ride. Struggling against suffering simply makes it worse. We are better off accepting suffering as part of life and realizing that all mortals take turns. The key is staying resilient and dealing with the issue. Situations have beginnings, middles, and ends. We solve for change and take the first step. Then the second, third, and fourth. Each step distances us from where we were and closer toward where we want to go.

Engage the third head

One big favor a crestfallen student, or anyone who finds him or herself down in the dumps, can do for him or herself is to temporarily park the noise and lock two of their three heads ("how they want to appear to others" and "how they do appear to others") in the closet. Revisit the third head (who, deep down, he or she truly is) and embrace that person.

This process of "mindfulness" frees the head and heart to get realigned, if not to a place of happiness then at least to place with enough clarity to see what's truly busted. Get rid of your biggest controllable Worry Circle issue. Do that, and you have already taken the first big step toward a better place.

Crowded heads rarely sleep well, and good sleep is vitally important to positive change. Exercise will help, as will mindful thought during sufficient, unplugged (non-digital) hours.

Each of us has bountiful gifts. By unlocking and removing the emotional handcuffs that prevent us from using those gifts we will be smarter and stronger next time, too. We will have acquired wisdom and learned resilience.

Emotional Intelligence

Resilience also benefits from emotional intelligence, which relies on the separation of facts and emotion. The online world is rife with opinion, which is worthless to a critical thinker. Facts matter, which means the search for and accumulation of facts-found online, offline, or both-enables us to draw independent conclusions rooted in reasons, not opinions. Facts help us learn and learning makes us stronger.

Smart people typically study on their own, not in groups, and these days finding information is simple. What is difficult is sifting through a data mountain to figure out what it all means. Collecting facts helps.

Formal education guarantees no one that he or she will excel at complex thinking and written communication. Identify an area of interest, whether related to problem solving, subject-matter expertise, or occupationally relevant insight, and strive to accumulate fact-based equity. The discipline of executing the search for fact-based information helps train the brain to analyze information and draw independent conclusions. Having experience with the fact-finding search process helps immensely when tough times call for resilience and action.

Why this matters

Fact-based thinking diffuses emotion by bringing a process driven approach and clarity to decision-making. The better we know ourselves, are able to separate the emotion of the moment from the facts at hand, evaluate options, and draw conclusions that inspire action, the more resilient we will be.

Resilience is a game-changer. Draw confidence and strength from becoming resilient, and trust that strength when times get tough. You will live to thrive another day and help others do the same.

Chapter 5

Summary & Final Thoughts

Technology's relentless encroachment into daily life is indisputable, as are signs of digital dependence, emotional reliance, and behavioral addiction. Noise is everywhere, relentlessly so for those who get lured in too far to proactively control behavioral decision-making and mind management.

What we do about these things-if anything-is up to us. We can treat our minds like castles and protect them by vigilant decision-making, do nothing and remain a pawn in a game that can hurt us but benefits others, or self-justify somewhere in between.

We are in ankle-deep water compared with the ocean we will be swimming in ten or twenty years from now. Machines will know more about us than family, friends, and loved ones. We will be subliminally barraged from relentless influence angles in multiple aspects of life. Behavioral persuasion is the mother lode-the future battleground-and robotic influence will progressively advance with Star Wars-like sophistication.

In the four decades I have observed, studied, researched, written about, and taught behavior and head management in business and collegiate circles, technology's catalytic force is unrivaled.

Nations, cultures, and people around the world are choosing (or being forced) to make different time choices. Some are beneficial, some are detrimental, but all are baby steps at the onset of a much longer, unpaved road to somewhere.

The key to thriving in our new reality will come from understanding why we do what we do, integrating awareness into prudent time choice decisions, and knowing how to monitor and regulate our emotions and feelings.

We can help our friends and families enormously by sharing what we have learned. Each of us is empowered to be a positive force in the lives of others. Embrace that opportunity. Doing so will enhance their lives and enrich yours as well.

Thank you for reading The Impact of Technology on Behavior & Happiness.

Best always,

Ocean Palmer

39706192R00126

Made in the USA
San Bernardino, CA
01 October 2016